# GHANA
## Understanding the People and their Culture

John Kuada and Yao Chachah

WOELI PUBLISHING SERVICES
ACCRA
1999

*Published by*
Woeli Publishing Services
P. O. Box NT 601
Accra New Town
Ghana

© John Kuada and Yao Chachah, 1999

ISBN 9964– 978 – 60– X
ISBN-13: 978-9964-978-60-0

Cover Design by George Siaw

*Marketed Overseas by*
African Books Collective
27 Park End Street,
Oxford OX1 1HU, UK

PRODUCED IN GHANA

Typeset by Woeli Publishing Services, Accra.

# Contents

# Preface

The notion that societies have distinct cultural values, norms and practices is now generally accepted in both academic and popular literature. Cross-cultural interactions have been found to have inherent potentials of conflict and must be carefully managed. An understanding of the cultures entered by foreigners is therefore seen as an important requirement for mutually rewarding cross-cultural interactions. We became vividly aware of the need for cultural knowledge through living in Denmark over nearly two decades.

The present book has therefore been motivated by the desire to help non-Ghanaians gain some understanding of the culturally prescribed rules of behaviour among Ghanaians. In so doing, we hope to ease the process of interaction between Ghanaians and foreigners and thereby contribute to the establishment of mutually beneficial interactions between them. We are, however, mindful of the fact that Ghanaians are remarkably tolerant and do not expect their guests to behave in a manner culturally prescribed for the local people. But Ghanaians show appreciation to foreigners who exhibit significant interest in their culture and make efforts to adjust to them.

The book was originally published in 1989 under the title: *Ghana — The Land, The People and Their Culture.* The present edition retains the main structure of the first one but elaborates on the concept of culture as applied in the book and presents a conceptual framework for exploring cultural differences. It also updates the political history of the country and draws attention to some aspects of daily life not included in the original version. The book provides a useful introduction to the country for people visiting Ghana for the first time. It also provides some explanation to events and behaviours that non-African foreigners are likely to find perplexing.

In writing this book we have immensely benefited from earlier published works on Ghanaian culture and lifestyle. We are very grateful to all these writers for the insights, directions and inspirations that their works have accorded us. We would also like to register our indebtedness to our parents for their initial cultural upbringing and to our wives and children in Denmark for teaching us the relevance of cultural understanding and adjustment in cross-cultural relationships. Without their constant encouragement, this book would not have been written.

Denmark, 1999                                JOHN KUADA
                                             YAO CHACHAH

# CHAPTER 1

# Introduction

Technological development during the last fifty years has made it increasingly possible for people all over the world to interact in a wide variety of ways. Travelling has, however, remained the most preferred method of learning about other places and people for a significant number of people. People visit Ghana for a wide range of reasons including business, project work, consultancy, research or tourism. Whatever the objective, the first-time visitor can hardly escape that chilly, creepy feeling of alienation, i.e. being without the familiar cues of life. The popular term for this feeling is *culture shock*. It starts with the unaccustomed senses of the new visitor quickly registering the basic, almost trivial elements in the environment — the distinctive smells, noises people make and how they gaze (or do not gaze) at each other during personal interactions. These initial impressions, however, fade quickly to the periphery of consciousness as visitors are submerged into the daily life of the community. They then begin to take note of more profound distinctive differences between their culture and that of their host society. For example, one begins to pay close attention to rituals associated with life-cycle events such as birth, puberty, marriage and death. The curious visitor then begins to ask for explanations underlying the rituals surrounding these rites of passage.

Cultural anthropologists have undertaken a systematic study of the manner in which societies in different parts of the world have chosen to organize their lives and collective understandings of their environment. Their main conclusion is that there are as many normal ways of thinking and acting in the world as there are societies, and one's own way of acting is not the only normal one. Although this book does not concern itself with an elaborate anthropological study of Ghanaian societies it is considered useful to draw the reader's attention to some of the perspectives and models that anthropologists use to explain the phenomenon — culture.

## Models of Culture

It is generally agreed that culture defines the relationships existing between people within a given community as well as between them and their environment. These relationships are based on a set of shared assumptions that develop over time to solve problems that people face both as social units and in their adaptation to physical environmental demands. It is therefore important to study culture relationally — i.e. with attention to multiple interconnections between the various cultural groups and members that constitute the focal culture.

Hofstede suggests that these relationships can be defined in terms of four dimensions:

(i) *Power distance* — indicating the extent to which a society accepts the fact that power in institutions and organizations is distributed unequally. The distribution of power in a society is reflected in the values of both the less powerful and the more powerful members of the society.

(ii) *Uncertainty avoidance* — indicating the extent to which a society feels threatened by uncertain and ambiguous situations and tries to avoid these situations by providing clearly defined rules to guide peoples' behaviour. Uncertainty avoidance may create a strong inner urge in people to work hard in order to protect themselves against eventualities in the future. Societies cope with uncertainty through various institutional frameworks, including technology, religion and law.

(iii)   *Individualism-Collectivism* — indicating whether the social framework in which people are supposed to take care of themselves is loosely or tightly knit.

(iv)   *Masculinity-Femininity* — indicating the extent to which the dominant values in the society are characterized by assertiveness, acquisition of money etc., or emphasize quality of life, sympathy and support for the disadvantaged.

Hofstede's four dimensional framework has been severely criticized for its simplicity (Neghandi, 1985) but has been extensively cited in the current literature for the same reason. The simplicity aside, Hofstede brings some of the critical factors that influence relations between groups of people in a given culture into focus.

Another model of culture that has gained popularity, particularly among Scandinavian scholars is that presented by Gullestrup (1992). He argues that, some of the immediately observable cultural institutions in a society include:

(i)   *Technology* — the mode of cultivation.

(ii)   *Economic systems*— the manner in which the society produces and distributes its goods and services.

(iii)   *Political institutions*— the dominant means of governance maintaining order and exercising power and authority in the society.

(iv)   *Association systems* — the mode of co-habitation and of social groupings that people form. This may range from fraternal and secret societies to professional or trade associations.

(v)   *Communication* — the mode of disseminating information, skills and knowledge.

(vi)   *Reproduction, socialization and education* — the mode of integration and development of individuals and groups.

(vii) *The ideological foundations of people's life* — i.e. the way of establishing and maintaining common identity.

(viii) *Religious systems* —That is the institutions forming the manifest characteristics of peoples' religious beliefs.

Underlying the observable institutions are what Gullestrup calls the vertical dimensions of culture. These include:

(i) *The underlying cultural structures,* i.e.the unwritten rules governing the patterns of socialization and inter-relationships between people of the society, for example, between women and men, the elders and the youth or between parents and children.

(ii) *Morals* i.e. the unwritten rules of how to behave under given situations.

(iii) *Values* i.e. beliefs that enable the members of the society to determine what is a desirable behaviour and what is not. Examples are: beauty/ugliness, honour/disgrace, guilt/innocence as well as the rules of fair play and obligations toward the family.

(iv) *Fundamental worldviews of the society,* i.e. philosophy of life or views that are generally held by members of the society as indisputable truths.

This perception broadens the concept of culture in the sense that dimensions normally treated as parallel to culture — i.e. political, economic and social institutions — are now brought under the cultural ambit and interactions clarified. The underlying characteristics of these elements are that they are collectively accepted and their usage is broad-based. For example, a piece of technological input used by a single individual within a community cannot by itself qualify as a cultural element since it is to have a limited impact on the behavioural pattern of the people of that community. But if its usage spreads, its impact

spreads concomitantly and   it may eventually end up being a
feature of an identified subculture of community or even become
a fundamental element of the macroculture as a whole.

Seen from a structural perspective, each cultural segment
will have a group of people who have vested interest in its
perpetuation. The degree of attachment to a particular cultural
segment will depend on the extent to which the segment contribu-
tes to the fulfilment of the interests and ambitions of the
individuals or groups concerned. The higher one's dependence
on the cultural segment, the higher the degree of attachment.
For example, while the priesthood and a few lay members of
a religion may advocate for the perpetuation of certain religious
rituals and traditions even if they retard economic and social
progress, other sections of the community may show less
enthusiasm for their preservation. There are also many examples
in history where political leaders align themselves with the
priesthood in order to impose their authority on the people they
govern. This argument suggests that even though the cultural
segments may seem to have equal importance in their functions,
their manipulation by interest groups in the society may alter
their relative influence from time to time.

**Key Features of Culture**

In summary, culture is generally described by the following
characteristics:

(i)  It is a *collective phenomenon*. Individuals may hold views
     that are at variance with the dominant cultural values
     and rules. Irrespective of how sensible and noble they
     may be from the  perspective of humanity in general,
     these personal views do not form part of the culture
     of their societies unless others adopt them. If adopted
     by a limited group of people, that group may constitute
     itself as a subcultural group.

(ii) It is a *product of time* or past behaviour or perception practised in the present. Some current behaviours of individuals in a given community may be classified as new and non-cultural. But if adopted and widely practised as time passes by, such behaviours will assume the status of culture. In other words, culture changes over time even starting with a single individual.

(iii) It is *acquired*, i.e. a learned behaviour. It therefore assumes a cognitive capacity of the cultural actors. The knowledge acquired influences the cultural actors' behaviour in an almost automatic fashion.

(iv) It is a *tenacious and unalterable phenomenon*. The more deeply-rooted and diffuse the values are, the more tenacious and unalterable the culture. This does not, however, deny the presence of undercurrents of change, stimulated by the unceasing process of social interaction within and without a given society.

## Aims and Structure of the Book

The cultural models and descriptions just outlined are not elaborately treated in the present book but are presented as a backcloth for viewing the issues discussed. The aim of this book is very simple. With it we hope to narrow the gap between what visitors may see in Ghana, how they may perceive them and the "reality" as perceived by Ghanaians themselves. The presentation, no doubt, leaves numerous holes for observant and motivated visitors to fill, and through this, enrich their memories of the visit. Since no academic treatment of the topics has been attempted, we provide a list of additional reading materials at the end for those who might wish a more detailed treatment of some of them. The reader is first introduced to Ghana and her inhabitants. In this section the vegetation, the tribes, the population and growth trends are described. The next section takes the reader through the historical, political and economic experiences of the people, describing their expectations, aspirations, frustrations as well as hopes for the future. A discussion of Ghanaian culture receives a significant weight. This section describes the total way of life of the people — reflecting their work and recreation, relations with the natural environment, attitudes and beliefs, values in life as well as the institutions that regulate their social relations.

The Ghanaian culture today is the result of a fusion of elements from accelerated local development and external stimuli, mainly contacts with Europe. The presentation in this book lays great emphasis on the traditional roots of the culture which still form the basis of behaviour among a greater part of the population, especially those living in the rural areas. The Western impacts, although not insignificant, can easily be observed and therefore require no elaborate description.

Good travelling is an art every traveller must cultivate if he or she has a genuine desire to learn something about other people's way of life. Travellers must always bear in mind that what enriches them can possibly rob or violate their hosts. No prescription is provided in this book that can serve as a good substitute for sensitivity to other people's feelings, perceptions and ways of life.

# CHAPTER 2

# Some Geographical and Demographic Characteristics

## Size and Location

The Republic of Ghana is located in the middle of the Guinea Coast between latitudes $4\frac{1}{2}^0$ North and $11\frac{1}{2}^0$ North. It is therefore quite close to the Equator. It is bordered to the east by Togo and to the west by Cote d'Ivoire. It also shares borders with Burkina Faso to the north while the Gulf of Guinea forms its southern border. It has a land area of 238,537 sq. km (92,100 sq. miles). The distance from the coast to its northern border is approximately 672 kilometres. The distance across the widest part from east to west is about 536 kilometres. This means that Ghana is about the size of United Kingdom and almost five times as big as Denmark. The coastal line is remarkably different from those of the neighbouring countries. It provides a number of natural harbours which, together with its natural resources, made the country a major trading centre on the West African Coast during the colonial period.

## Landscape

A visitor travelling by air will readily notice that the land is generally flat, with only a few mountains and plateaus which do not reach very high. These elevations are richly covered with verdant tropical vegetation which provides them with a beauty refreshing to the eyes. The coastal area consists of lagoons and sandy bays which are gradually replaced by low-lying plains extending about 30 km  inland. Northwards, the landscape becomes more varied with gently rising hills. A series of hills called the Akwapim ranges lie between Akuapim and Winneba. These ranges generally have deep and narrow valleys and can be seen from Accra in the northern horizon. Much of the central and north-eastern part of the country is covered by large plateaus of flat lying rocks. Geographers call this area the Volta Basin.

There are also a large number of cataracts, rapids, falls, rivers and lakes which offer additional variations in scenic attraction. The most famous and better known falls are the Begoro and Boti falls, both in the Eastern Region of the country and Wli waterfall in the Volta Region. Similarly,  Lake Bosomtwi stands out prominently among the natural lakes. It is the largest natural lake situated about 33 km south-east of Kumasi. It is formed by a circular depression surrounded by a deep and enormous steep-sided crater. Its total area is about 48 sq. km. In parts it reaches depths of 72 metres. It is a popular tourist attraction. The Black and White Volta rivers flow into the country from Burkina Faso, joining each other in the northern region of Ghana to become the largest river in Ghana. With the building of the Akosombo dam (to generate electricity) in the mid-1960s, the Volta River was turned into an artificial lake, becoming one of the largest man-made lakes in the world.

## Climate and Vegetation

Broadly speaking the country can be divided into two climatic regions — the south and the north — with some variations in each region. The vegetation is accordingly determined by the climatic conditions in each region. There are two rainy seasons in the southern part of the country (April–June and September – November). The annual rainfall here varies between 127 cm and 210 cm. The coastal areas experience lighter rains with annual rainfall in Accra averaging only 71 cm. As a result, the coastal vegetation is a treeless grassland with occasional shrubs and mangroves at the mouth of the lagoons. The heaviest rainfalls occur in the south-western corner of the country, with annual rainfalls averaging 210 cm. Naturally, the typical rainforests are found in this area. The Ashanti–Kwahu highlands of the north-western region also register considerable rainfalls. The maximum rainfalls in this area are around June–October, averaging about 140 cm annually.

The southern part is also characterized by generally humid conditions throughout the year. In the coastal zone, the relative humidity reaches between 95 and 100 percent at night. It is, however, relatively low during the harmattan season which starts in December and ends in January. The northern half of the country covers an area of almost 150,000 sq. km, and comprises short trees and grass. This area experiences only one rainy season in April–September with annual averages of 110-127 cm. The temperature is generally uniform all over the country. Average temperatures are between 26°C and 29°C, with the highest temperatures experienced in the northern region between February and April, usually just before the start of the rainy season.

## The People

The movement of people into areas around northern Ghana started about 4,000 years ago. Their number was very small and like most other people of that period, they lived by hunting and food gathering. The improved knowledge of farming techniques and iron tools which developed during the period enabled some of the people to move closer to the forest regions. Tribal communities began to emerge about 2,000 years ago. The Guan groups occupied parts of the north, the Accra Plains and the Volta River Valley; the Vagala, the Sisala and the Tallensi groups occupied the north.

The population has increased rapidly since the 13th century when vigorous trading activities (particularly in gold) made the area exceptionally attractive to people living in the neighbouring countries. Today five major tribal communities live in Ghana, in addition to many smaller ones interspersed among them. They are the Akan, the Ga-Adangme, the Ewe, the Gonja and the Mole-Dagbani, each composed of many distinct ethnic groups. (About 100 ethnic groups were listed in the 1960 census.) All of these groups speak languages of the Niger-Congo language family and share cultural characteristics with other West African communities. As mentioned earlier, the country can be divided roughly into two climatic zones — drier savannah flatlands of the north and a dense vegetation zone of the south. This broad climatic zoning coincides with the locations of the main ethnic communities of the country. The Akan, the Ga-Adangme, and the Ewe ethnic communities live in the south while the Gonja and the Mole-Dagbani people live in the north. Members of the Akan ethnic community constitute about 44% of the total population, Mole-Dagbani 16%, Ewe 13%, Ga-Adangme 8% and Gonja 4%. Since the ethnic communities provide their members with a common language as well as a spiritual root and a common way of life, they serve to bring people with distant blood relations into a wider sociological relationship (Assimeng, 1981). Apart from the family, tribes provide their members with a common identity and some temporary emotional release from the strains and anxieties of the daily life.

The southern communities, particularly those along the coastal belt, have had the longest and the most far-reaching contacts with western religion and education. For example, schools in the coastal south were established (mostly by missionaries) at least sixty to eighty years earlier than in the north. Many of the southern communities are therefore predominantly Christians. The first batch of the country's intellectuals and professionals also come from these communities, the majority of them coming from Fante (Akan) and Ga communities located along the coastal areas. The northern communities have been influenced mainly by Islam through their pre-colonial trading relations with Arabs. Their contact with western institutions is therefore of relatively recent origin.

Ghana can therefore be termed a multi-ethnic country, each ethnic community having its own history of migration, specific customs, values and rules of behaviour. Until recently, geographical mobility within the country has been considerably limited and the spatial isolation of the various ethnic communities has resulted in stereotype perceptions of one another. Many of these stereotypes have hitherto survived the increased geographical mobility and interactions in present-day Ghana. Thus the Ewes are labelled as jujumen (practitioners of "black magic"), the Asantes as aggressive, the Fantes as westernized and the Kwahus as business/money-conscious. It must be stressed, however, that these stereotypes hardly reflect the reality of the dominant profiles of these communities today. Although the ethnic identities are still firmly maintained, several years of political appeal for unity and the spatial mobility of the population in general have reduced incidents of overt inter-ethnic conflicts in the country.

*The Akan*

The Akan groups form the majority of the population (over 44%). They migrated from the Chad-Benue regions and settled first at the confluence of the Pra and the Offin Rivers in the forest region of Ghana, around the 11th century. Over the years they developed a distinctive language, institutions and customs by which they are now identified as a tribe. Some of the groups moved northwards while others moved southwards forming kingdoms or states of their own. The most distinctive groups today include the Fante living in the south-western coastal region, the Asante in the forest region, the Akwapim in the south-east and the Brong Ahafo in the north-west. All the Akan groups have a common calendar, common religious beliefs, and a matrilineal system of inheritance, i.e. they belong to their mother's clan. They speak dialects of the Akan language, the major ones being Twi and Fante.

*The Ga-Adangme*

The Ga-Adangme groups live in the coastal plains stretching from Accra to Tema. They migrated from Yorubaland in southern Nigeria in the 14th century. After crossing the Volta River, the Adangme group settled on the coast (west of the river) while the Ga group moved to the Accra plains. Here they met part of the Guan groups who were already settled in the area. The Ga people subsequently conquered the Guan and absorbed them into their community. (The people of present-day Sempe are descendants of the Guan.) Like the Akan, the Ga and Adangme people developed their own languages, customs and traditions which distinguish them from other tribes of the country. Although the languages spoken by the two groups are related, they are mutually unintelligible. There are also a number of other cultural differences between the Ga and the Adangme peoples, due in part to the influence of the Akan on the Ga people and of the Ewe on the Adangme people. The Ga became very prosperous during the 17th century through trading with the Europeans. They established themselves as a powerful kingdom composed of many smaller states. These include the present groups in central Accra *(Ga Mashi)*, and those in Osu, Labadi, Teshie, Nungua and Tema. These groups are essentially independent and have their own chiefs *(Mantse)* and systems of administration.

*The Ewe*

The Ewe live in the area south-east of the Volta Lake. Some groups of the tribe also occupy the southern half of the Republics of Togo and Benin. When the Yoruba empire began to expand, there was a serious shortage of land. This forced the Ewe to migrate, around the 16th century, in search of a new home. One group of the migrants crossed the Volta at the south and settled in the lowland regions east of the river. Another group settled in the coastal plains and the third settled in the north-west where a section of the Guan tribe — the Avatime and Kposso people— already lived. The settlements rapidly grew into states and the prestige of their leaders increased. By 1900 there were as many as 120 Ewe states spread over a wide area of the Volta Basin. The Ewe people adopted a policy of mutual co-existence with the Guan tribal groups who had come before them. The latter continued to live independently retaining their own languages and culture. But over time, many of them have learnt Ewe as a second language and have adopted some Ewe cultural practices.

### The Northern Tribes: Mole-Dagbani and Gonja

The founders of the Mole-Dagbani tribes (sometimes called the Mossi-Grunshi tribes) came from the east of the Chad Lake towards the end of the 15th century. Their military superiority enabled them to defeat the existing tribal groups in the north — i.e. Vagala, the Sisala and the Tampulensi — and to impose their authority on them. Their first leader, Gbewa was succeeded as king by his eldest son, Zirile. But after the death of Zirile, dispute on the question of succession broke between his eldest surviving brother, Tohogu and his younger brothers. The dispute led to a civil war and a subsequent split within the tribe. Tohogu and his supporters formed the kingdom of Mamprugu. His subjects took the name Mamprusi. His younger brothers formed the kingdoms of Dagomba and Nanumba. But since the kingdoms share a common ancestral root, they are considered as one tribe and are called the Mole-Dagbani people. The founders of the Gonja tribe migrated from Mali and arrived in their present area around the end of the 16th century. They defeated the scattered groups of the Guan tribe they encountered and founded a new kingdom. After consolidating their rule, they successfully waged wars against tribes within the locality and expanded their territorial influence. In the 17th and much of the 18th centuries, the Gonja constituted one of the major kingdoms in the north. Their military successes were, however, reversed in the 19th century, by the Asante, to whom they became a tributary. By the time of independence, the Gonja were mostly migrant workers — working in other parts of the country.

**Urbanization and Inter-Ethnic Relations**

A notable development in the social and ethnic structure of the country during the past forty years is the migration of rural dwellers to urban areas. Cities such as Kumasi and Accra are no longer inhabited only by the original ethnic communities of the areas. For example, as far back as 1955, Asantes numbered only 45% of the inhabitants of Kumasi, the main city of the Asante people (Austin, 1976).

Migration to the urban areas has markedly influenced many Ghanaians' aspirations in life and expectations from their families and communities. Compared to the rural communities, the towns and cities are more open, and the social structures are more fluid and dynamic. The multi-ethnicity of the towns and the emergence of many new professional groups remove some of the hindrances to social mobility. Admission into new rewarding associations and social networks has become possible without prejudice to the advantages that familism and ethnicity provide. Thus the achieved status positions of such professionals as lawyers, doctors, accountants as well as senior civil servants and politicians now compete effectively (and in some communities overshadow) the ascribed status positions found in the traditional communities.

Urbanization and the increased socio-economic expectations have brought in their trail a change in the basis of evaluating prestige in the Ghanaian society in general. The number of wives and children as a yardstick of social status has been replaced by conspicuous consumption in the form of fancy cars, expensive clothing and membership of exclusive western associations such as Rotary and Masons (Assimeng, 1981). The hitherto modest traditional rites such as outdooring, wedding and funeral ceremonies have been given a new status of glamour and pomp as marks of social distinction and status differences. People in similar positions or of similar levels of education are compared with each other within the broader community on the basis of their display of wealth.

Ordinary Ghanaians have not escaped the influence of such conspicuous show of wealth by the few privileged ones in the urban areas. A general redefinition of peoples' expectations of themselves as well as the roles and obligations of their more prosperous family members has emerged. A senior position in government office or any work organization is seen by the near and distant family members of the incumbent as an opportunity for social mobility. These expectations have been reinforced during the past three decades by the shrinking economic opportunities in the country as a whole.

Doubtlessly, the economic changes of the past four decades have radically influenced the Ghanaian culture in many ways. People now talk of traditional and modern patterns of life and most Ghanaians participate in both and try, sometimes unsuccessfully at times to enjoy the benefits of both. The quality of life that the so-called traditional culture offers them (i.e. mental stability, protection and emotional satisfaction) are now seriously eroded by their perceived relative deprivation. The vast majority of less fortunate ones that are unable to enjoy the benefits of economic prosperity are visibly frustrated and some seek the help of the gods and spirits to succeed while others resign, seeking solace in christian promises of the paradise hereafter.

## Dominant Patterns of Life

Although contacts with Western culture, which are pronounced in the urban areas, have created opportunities for achieved status mobilities and patterns of behaviour, most Ghanaians still remain firmly attached to their traditional cultural roots. Role definitions based on ascriptions and other traditional prerogatives have not been entirely obliterated even in the urban areas, and much less in the rural areas. Recruitment to traditional political offices (e.g. chiefs) is still based on descent, and the exercise of authority remains validated by traditional religious beliefs. An example of this is the profound veneration for ancestors by family members. In general terms, it is believed that ancestors look over their descendants and in reciprocation are propitiated. Thus customary rites of passage and propitiation of ancestors are taken seriously, even in communities where the details of such rites have been modified as a result of cultural change.

The influence of traditional values on the acculturation process is eminently seen in the relationship between elders and their juniors. In the rural areas in particular, children are still expected to maintain a low profile in the presence of their seniors in age. They must not argue with their seniors let alone quarrel. As Assimeng (1981, p. 74) observes "almost invariably, when children quarrelled with elders, children were adjudged guilty, not so much because of the substantive nature of the case, but because it is held to be impudence and uncustomary behaviour for children to dare challenge their elders in public." The prominence of age as an ascribed social status in Ghana is demonstrated in a popular Akan proverb that *"Yewo panyin ansa na yeawo ohene,"* literally meaning "the elder was born before even the chief."

In summary, Ghana may be described as a plural society. Luckily, however, the distinctive ethnic groups have co-existed over 500 years and their interactions have achieved higher degrees of intensity in more recent years without the negative consequences of domination, conflict and instability as seen in some other plural societies. The ethnic communities, particularly the new generations that have lived in the urban areas, appear to have accepted the benefits of mutual co-existence which have so far held in check remnants of suspicion. There is an increasing rate of inter-ethnic marriages today, particularly among the educated urban dwellers, often with the blessings of their parents and grandparents.

# CHAPTER 3

# A Brief Political History

The first Europeans, the Portuguese arrived on the Gold Coast in 1471. Their enthusiasm to establish an enduring relationship with the people grew rapidly due to the enormous trading opportunities the area presented. On the strength of this, they negotiated with the local chiefs of Elmina for the construction of a fort. Eleven years later, in 1482, the construction of Fort San Jorge d'Elmina was completed, thereby becoming the first European building on the Gold Coast. This was followed by Fort San Antonio, built at Axim in 1515, and Fort San Sebastian at Shama in.1526. With these forts, the Portuguese were able to establish a dominant trading post on the Gold Coast for over a century. Their interest was primarily of a commercial nature. They did not attempt to conquer the land or to take possession of it by any other means. The relationship they established with the local inhabitants served as an unwritten guideline for later arrivals until the beginning of the 19th century.

The French, the Dutch, the Danes and the British arrived around the end of the 16th century. About the same time, the harbours and ports in Spain and Portugal were closed to Dutch traders due to a conflict between Holland and Spain. The Dutch retaliated by attacking the Portuguese trading posts in different parts of the world, including those on the Gold Coast. They captured Fort San Jorge d'Elmina in 1637, and by 1642 the remaining two forts were also captured, thus bringing a crushing end to the Portuguese trading activities on the Gold Coast.

By the 17th century, the Gold Coast became famous not only for its gold but also for slaves. The rapid expansion of the plantation economies of the West Indian Islands led to an increased demand for slaves to which the Gold Coast traders responded with vigour. The scramble for slaves resulted in persistent confusion and conflict among the traders as well as among the local people. Firearms were brought into the country in generous quantities, most of them finding their way into the hands of rival local communities, and thereby indirectly stimulating military confrontations among them. The period was also marked by the construction of numerous lodges, forts and castles which served as protection against the frequent cannon wars fought among the Europeans. The forts and castles also served as prisons for slaves awaiting shipment.

## The Colonial Era

The loss of American colonies in the 18th century reduced the British slave market considerably, and marked the beginning of a new British policy on the Gold Coast and Africa as a whole. The new class of British industrialists looked to Africa for raw materials and a new market for their mass produced goods rather than for slaves. The British parliament, bowing to pressure from both their industrialists and humanitarian public opinion in and outside Britain, passed an act in 1807 which made trade in slaves illegal. The Dutch, under British pressure, followed suit.

With the abolition of the slave trade, the cost of administering the forts and trading posts quickly outweighed the incomes from the remaining trading activities. Some traders invested in productive undertakings such as farming to compensate for the loss but without success. The only reasonable economic decision left under the circumstances was to pull out. The Danes sold all their possessions to the British for £10,000 in 1850 and left. The Dutch also left in 1872, leaving the British in control of the trading activities in the country.

Even before the departure of the European traders, the British were preparing themselves legally and administratively to assume political control over the Gold Coast. In 1821, Sir Charles MacCarthy was appointed the first Governor of the crown over the territories which were already under the control of British traders. Arriving to assume his duties on 27 March 1822, he immediately proclaimed the territories a colony, and extended British military protection to the smaller local states which were persistently harassed by the militarily superior Asante kingdom. On 6 March 1844, the British signed a treaty with a number of Fante chiefs in which the latter were also guaranteed British protection against attacks from the Asante. In return, these Fante communities also came under the British colonial administration. This treaty, popularly known as the Bond of 1844, marked the beginning of the formal colonial rule over a greater part of the Gold Coast. It is therefore not a sheer coincidence that the independence of Ghana came to fall on 6 March 1957 (113 years later).

The Asante aggressions did not come to an end until they were defeated by the British in a series of wars during the second half of the 19th century. In 1901 the Asante kingdom was finally annexed to the British Gold Coast Colony. The other parts of the country were also gradually absorbed during the succeeding two decades.

## The Struggle for Independence

The British consolidated the reins of their administration over the local population during the early decades of the 20th century. The functions of government which were traditionally performed by chiefs went to civil servants appointed by the Crown. Laws were passed to regulate commercial and civil life. But the local chiefs and their subjects never gave up the fight to remain independent. They protested vigorously against laws which were considered an encroachment on the rights of the local inhabitants. One of these notorious laws was The Lands Bill of 1894. The bill was ostensibly aimed at preventing local citizens from giving lands not belonging to them to European concessionaires. However, its content and wording aroused suspicion among some local lawyers, who believed it was a British attempt to take away the land from the true owners, namely the local citizens. Consequently the Aborigines Rights Protection Society (ARPS) was formed to channel formal protest to the British government. This marked the beginning of 60 years of organized nationalist agitation on the Gold Coast.

The nationalist groups which subsequently emerged, constituted themselves into watchdogs of national interest. They protested initially only against what they considered to be injustices of the colonial administration — e.g. lack of economic opportunities for the local citizens, restrictions on cultural practices and naked exploitation of the country's natural resources. Later on, they began to demand representation of local citizens on the law making body with the conviction that it was the only way they could exert positive and significant influences on the socio-economic situation of the people. But the British did not feel compelled to hasten constitutional change in the Gold Coast. Minor reforms were made; e.g. local citizens were appointed to administrative posts, and few schools were established. By 1916, three local inhabitants had also been awarded seats on the Legislative Council.

The real struggle for independence began after World War II with the formation of political parties. The ordinary people were then organized for demonstrations and other popular political actions. The hectic political agitations of this period forced the British to agree to the demands for independence. As a result, parliamentary elections were held in 1951 and again in 1956. In both cases, the Convention People's Party (CPP) won convincingly, thereby removing any doubts in the minds of the British about the preparedness of the people to govern themselves.

On 6 March 1957 the Gold Coast was declared independent

by the British in a wave of grea... ɔpular enthusiasm. Dr. Kwame Nkrumah, the dynamic leader and founder of the CPP became the first Prime Minister of the first decolonized country south of the Sahara. The stage was set for a new life, full of hopes and expectations. The expectations of the people and their new leaders were symbolically captured in the new name given to the country — GHANA.

## The Name Ghana

The name, Ghana has deep roots in African history. Historical records show that a remarkable and powerful kingdom blossomed in the savannah belt south of the Sahara during the 7th century. This kingdom was called Ghana. It was described with great respect in all the accounts of such Arabian writers as Al-Fazari and Al-Bakri. The kingdom was copiously rich and its administration as well as social infrastructure (i.e. schools and health services) were generously praised. In other words, the kingdom was a concrete testimony of what the emerging nations of Africa could do. This message came to the people of the Gold Coast loud and clear on the day of their independence. The name Ghana was chosen as an inspiration towards the future.

## Post-Independence Political and Economic Changes

Ghana has experienced a chequered political history since independence. Its civilian governments have witnessed quick exits. The military has led the country for a combined period of 20 years. It has assigned itself the task of protecting the citizens against the civilian regimes. Ghanaians have been "liberated" in 1966, by the National Liberation Council from the dictatorship of the Nkrumah government; "redeemed" in 1972 by the National Redemption Council (of Acheampong) from the corrupt and inefficient Busia administration. In 1979 the Armed Forces

Revolutionary Council inspired a revolt against the corruption of Acheampong's military government. In 1981 the Provisional National Defence Council of Rawlings toppled the Limann government. Since then, the country has enjoyed a stable administration under the leadership of Jerry John Rawlings who successfully turned his military regime into a civilian one. All along, Ghanaians have waited silently, patiently and hopefully for a better day. The following sections provide a quick review of events since 1981.

As noted earlier, the first civilian government of the Convention People's Party (CPP) headed by Kwame Nkrumah was elected on the wave of popular nationalistic feelings and expectations. These expectations were shattered when the economy crumbled and the country was placed under one-party state leadership with despotic tendencies. The political experiment under the CPP was also characterized by conditional allegiance under which politicians tried to bind their followers to their cause and vision through an orchestrated network of group interests and individual patronage. As Austin (1976, p. 41) reports "CPP candidates who lost the 1956 elections were given diplomatic appointments abroad, directorships on the public corporations, jobs in the Workers' Brigade or Regional Commissioners' offices or scholarships to study law." This practice became a foundational element of Ghanaian political culture during the subsequent years and regimes.

Naturally, political independence did not fulfil all the economic and social expectations of the people. Significant progress was made in the fields of education, health and other social services. But economic progress was slow. Many state-owned industries were established only to remain unproductive due to lack of inputs. In addition, the civilian leaders began to place their personal interests above the common good of the nation. The corruption of public officers, poor economic management and mounting foreign debts created grave economic problems. Already in the early 1960s the country began to experience serious shortages of basic commodities and extremely high prices for the few goods available.

These observations are, however, not peculiar to Ghana. Evidence of distributory politics and political patronage has been noted in several other African countries (Jones, 1986; Leonard, 1987; Montgomery, 1987; Reilly, 1989). For example, Reilly (1989, p.176) argues that "It is the political and social influences on management development that provide the key to the problem (of unimproved management performance in Africa)." Similarly, Leonard (1987) sees political rationalities as underlying the economic irrationalities found in Africa.

The economic problems of the early 1960s and the lack of public confidence in the civilian leaders provided the military with justifications to overthrow the Nkrumah government in a *coup d'état* led by Lt. Col. (later, General) Kotoka on 24 February 1966. This marked the beginning of direct military involvement in the political life of the country. The NLC ruled Ghana for three and a half years. The economy did not recover during this period. It actually deteriorated; the rate of inflation was high and basic commodities remained extremely scarce.

But the government perhaps had good reasons not to worry. Right from the outset the NLC saw itself as a transitional government. The main aim of the leaders was to prepare the country for her next civilian government. A new constitution was drawn up in 1969 and parliamentary elections were held during the same year. The elections were overwhelmingly won by the Progress Party (PP) led by Dr. K.A. Busia. Busia became the second civilian Prime Minister of Ghana, enjoying enthusiastic support which made him resolve not to repeat the errors of the past.

The weak economy, however, remained a major stumbling block to progress. Foreign debts inherited from the Nkrumah era continued to grow steadily while world market prices for the country's major export crop (cocoa) continued to fall. The net result was a continued shortage of imported inputs and basic commodities including drugs and spare parts. Investment in economic and social infrastructure suffered severely. At the same time, generous additions were made to the population and the fascinations of urban forms of life were luring young people to the towns and cities to swell the unemployment numbers. The inevitable consequence was naked poverty and widespread social dissatisfaction.

The Busia government became overwhelmed by the magnitude of the problems. It failed to produce a coherent and effective economic policy that could reduce the socio-economic hardships. As a result, the government quickly ran into serious political difficulties. Once again a justification was trumped up for a military intervention. The acting commander of a unit of the army Col. (later, General) Kutu Acheampong overthrew the Busia government on 13 January 1972 and formed the country's second military government which was named the National Redemption Council (NRC).

The economic problems grew worse under the NRC regime. As Loxley (1988) reports, real GDP per capita first stagnated and then fell steadily from the early 1970s onwards. The stagnation or decline was evident in all the productive sectors of the economy. Between 1970 and 1984, for example, it was estimated that value added within the agricultural sector fell by 14%; manufacturing by 43%, mining by 17% and construction by 37%. The food self-sufficiency ratio fell from 83 in the mid-1960s to 71 in the late 1970s and to only 62 in 1982. Merchandise exports has fallen steadily in both volume and value since 1970. Capacity utilization fell to 20%–25% in most manufacturing enterprises, mainly due to the lack of foreign currency to import raw materials and other inputs. The state budget was consequently destabilized as a result of the low ebb of economic activities. For example, cocoa duty which accounted for 37% of government revenues and grants in 1970 fell to 0.8 percent of the 1980 real value. At the same time the population was growing at an annual rate of 3% and the urban population at about 5%. The pressure on the supply of all goods and services led to a rapid rate of inflation which reached 120% annually in the early 1980s.

A vast majority in the Ghanaian society experienced substantial reductions in real income in the 1970s. Thousands of highly educated Ghanaians left the country to look for jobs wherever they could find one. For those who stayed on, the inflationary erosion of their purchasing power meant that monthly salaries barely could cover a week's living cost. Illicit means of raising money such as theft, corruption and black marketing also became more common. The ultimate consequence of this dismal economic climate was the decline of moral probity within Ghanaian work organizations. Public property became euphemistically termed *aban dea*, (an Akan expression meaning "It is for the government") with the connotation of a "free good". This, by inference, means that such properties can be stolen, abused or destroyed with no direct consequence to the individual. The machinery of control within the public sector has also been rendered non-operative since those who would normally be expected to enforce the formal rules of behaviour are also involved in the practice.

In addition to this, huge cuts in budget allocations to schools, hospitals and health centres as well as to the maintenance of roads and transport systems resulted in a deterioration in public sector services in general. Frustrations among workers in these sectors, both as a result of the decline in their personal living standards and their inability to provide the services for which they had been trained meant work morals were very low. These conditions further accentuated the problems of indifference and irresponsibility in work organizations.

As the situation continued to deteriorate, the university students joined the professional bodies in the country to agitate for a return to civilian rule. At the same time internal rivalries within the NRC itself began to sap the energies of the government. Acheampong tried to solve the problems by dissolving the NRC's executive council and replacing it with a seven-member Supreme Military Council (SMC). This cosmetic change did not soften the political mood of the general population. In a further attempt to avoid a popular uprising, the SMC removed its leader, Acheampong, and replaced him with General Akuffo, the then Chief-of-Defence-Staff. Nevertheless the disturbances continued and with greater intensity with each passing day. Rumours of discontent among the junior officers of the military circulated while the government members were openly accused of corruption and mismanagement. The patience of the ordinary Ghanaian seemed to be reaching its full exhaustion. This atmosphere of confusion and frustration provided another opportunity for a military intervention. A group of young soldiers led by Flt. Lt. J. J. Rawlings seized power in a *coup d'état* which was greeted with almost a universal cry of relief. The Armed Forces Revolutionary Council (AFRC) was thus formed as Ghana's third military government on 4 June 1979, with Flt. Lt. J. J. Rawlings as the chairman and head of state.

The AFRC set itself the task of instilling a high degree of moral attitude, concern and discipline into the political leadership of the country. Eight top political and military leaders, including Acheampong and Akuffo, were tried on charges of corruption and mismanagement and executed by firing squad between 16 and 26 June 1979. But the AFRC's "house cleaning" exercise did not disturb the programme for return to civilian rule. Parliamentary elections were held on 18 June 1979 and on 9 July presidential elections were also held. The People's National Party (PNP) which won these elections formed Ghana's third civilian government in September 1979, with its leader Dr. Hilla Limann as the new President.

Despite seemingly serious and constructive efforts, Limann's government had not much luck with the economy. Internal party rivalries also drained a great deal of its zeal and energy. By the beginning of 1981 there were again visible signs of a political crisis. A number of notable PNP leaders were accused of corruption. Efforts were made to purge the leadership through dismissals, but by the end of 1981 the authority of the PNP became seriously eroded. Limann was seen by the ordinary Ghanaian as an ineffective leader.

Rawlings led another successful *coup d'état* on 31 December 1981 and formed the Provisional National Defence Council (PNDC) as Ghana's fourth military government. Initially, the PNDC's political efforts appeared to usher Ghanaians into a new era of hope. The government's emphasis was on the involvement of the ordinary citizens in the decision-making bodies of the country through the formation of Citizens' Defence Committees and Workers' Defence Committees. The understanding behind the formation of these committees was that ordinary Ghanaians will be encouraged to shoulder the task of national reconstruction once they have been given the power to make their own decisions. But these expectations were belied. In 1992, under the pressure of the international community, particularly the major aid donor countries, Rawlings agreed to return the country to democratic rule. He contested and won the presidential election in November 1992 as a leader of the National Democratic Congress (NDC). The NDC won 189 of the 200 seats in the Legislature a month later. He was re-elected in December 1996 for a second term. Rawlings' two successive election victories after 10 years of his military leadership has been greeted approvingly by the international community which has invested so much energy and prestige in the rejuvenation of the Ghanaian economy. The reasoning is that despite the evident economic weaknesses in recent years, the Rawlings government still represents the best guarantor for continued stability.

More neutral political commentators have described

Rawlings' period of government until now as characterized by both stability and flux. Under him, Ghana has witnessed the longest period of unchanged government since Nkrumah, thereby providing the country with political stability. At the same time he has not been able to fulfil the needs and aspirations of most Ghanaians, a promise he made on the day he grabbed power for the second time. The question asked, however, by many political commentators is whether the 15 years of Rawlings administration has ushered Ghana into a period of political stability and economic growth. Has Rawlings a clear-cut political agenda and a coherent economic programme or will he fall prey to the mishaps that have befallen regimes before him? As we ponder over this question we need to remind ourselves of the general view that African governments are more interested in survival rather than development. As one commentator puts it: "In African countries governance is more a matter of seamanship and less one of navigation — that is staying afloat rather than going somewhere." It has been claimed that Rawlings fell prey to the temptation of "staying afloat" during the 1992 elections by overspending and temporarily disrupting the economic progress the country made in the 1980s. He seems to have resisted the temptation during the 1996 elections, a sign of political maturity.

## A Note About Human Rights

Before we leave the description of Ghana's political history, it is worth informing the reader about the human rights records during the four decades of independence. The later years of the Nkrumah regime (1960–1966) were noted for flagrant abuse of human rights. He instituted a single party system and declared himself life president. He was reputed for running the country as if it were his personal property, making and un-making laws at his discretion, the notorious one among them being the

Preventive Detention Act (PDA). The act enabled the police to arrest any person who seemingly disapproved any government action or decision. Many politically active citizens found themselves in jail under the PDA. The 1966 coup was therefore legitimized as an act to free Ghanaians from the abuse of individual liberty and civil rights.

Under the successive military governments as well, some military personnel misused their power and positions in utter disregard for basic human rights. Property ownership was either regarded with scorn or suspicion; honest citizens who earned their wealth genuinely did not escape the atrocities of the soldiers. It was not unusual for vehicles, houses and money to be confiscated "in the service of the revolution". The victims remained usually calm for fear of provoking the soldiers even further. Ebow Daniel (1993) reports of an instance in which a military officer demanded the keys of a brand new limousine from the owner for it to be used for "operations". He hesitated until a slap landed on one cheek, another on the other. He made to fight but surrended the keys instead, "as if just remembering a man had only two cheeks, or that when both cheeks have been pressed into service in a 'just' cause there was not much more to do. For days the limousine had not been returned and both cheeks still smarted." This is just one of the many similar instances that the relatively well-to-do of the society experienced during the heat of the "revolutions".

## MAJOR POLITICAL EVENTS WORTH KNOWING

1471  Portuguese navigators arrived on the Gold Coast
1482  The Elmina Castle was built
1553  The British began trading on the Gold Coast
1595  The Dutch began trading on the Gold Coast
1623  The Danes built Christiansborg Fort
1631  The British built a lodge at Cormantin

1637  The Dutch captured the Elmina Castle
1642  The Dutch took over all Portuguese possessions
1645  The Christiansborg fort was captured by the Swedes
1652  The Swedes built a castle at Cape Coast
1661  The Christiansborg fort was built into a castle by the Danes
1752  The African Company of Merchants was formed
1807  Slave trade was made illegal
1818  British mission to the Asante
1821  British government took control of the administration of their territory on the Gold Coast, placing it under Sierra Leone
1824  The British were defeated by the Asante; Governor Sir Charles MacCarthy was killed
1826  The Asante were defeated at Dodowa
1828  Administration of British territories was returned to British merchants
1843  The British government resumed control over the territories
1844  "The Bond of 1844" was signed on 6 March
1850  Administration of British (Gold Coast) territories was separated from Sierra Leone
1852  First meeting of the Legislative Council
1866  The Gold Coast was again placed under Sierra Leone government
1872  Dutch possessions sold to the British
1873  The Asante were defeated at Elmina
1874  Final separation from Sierra Leone
1896  Prempeh I, King of Asante was deported to Seychelles
1897  Protectorate was formally declared over the Northern Territories
1901  The Asante were formally annexed
1925  Prempeh I returned, now as an ordinary citizen
1927  Achimota college and school was opened
1928  Takoradi harbour opened

1946 "Burns" Constitution

1947 United Gold Coast Convention (UGCC) was founded by G. A. Grant

1948 General political disturbances

1948 The Watson Commission was appointed

1949 The Coussey Committee was appointed

1949 CPP was founded by Dr. Kwame Nkrumah

1951 Dr. Kwame Nkrumah was made leader of government

1952 Dr. Kwame Nkrumah became first Prime Minister of the Gold Coast

1954 All African Legislative Assembly

1957 Ghana became independent (6 March)

1960 Ghana became Republic (1 July)

1966 The first military intervention (NLC formed – 24 February)

1969 Return to civilian government with Dr. K. A. Busia as Prime Minister

1972 The second military intervention (NRC formed on 13 January)

1979 The third military intervention (AFRC formed on 4 June)

1979 Return to civilian government with Dr. Hilla Limann as President (September)

1981 The fourth military intervention (PNDC formed with Flt. Lt. J. J. Rawlings as Chairman and Head of State)

1993 The Return to civilian government with Jerry John Rawlings as President

1997 Jerry John Rawlings starts a second term as President.

# CHAPTER 4

# Recent Economic Experience

The macro-economic strategies pursued in Ghana since independence were influenced by both the mainstream economic development thoughts of the day and the political ambitions of the leaders of the country. The heightened expectations that pre-independence nationalist agitations brought about compelled politicians to hurry the pace of economic growth after independence. Jobs had to be created, infrastructure developed and dependence on imports reduced. These socio-economic demands led to the rapid establishment of state enterprises and the nationalization of the few private ones. The public service sector was equally enlarged to accommodate the administrative requirements of the economic development experiments.

The rapidity with which the organizations were created had two major negative consequences on management. Firstly, there was an acute dearth of skilled managerial staff to fill the various vacancies. Many of them were filled with less qualified people who, as already noted, were offered the jobs as a token of gratitude for or in lieu of political favours. The organizational cultures existing in many Ghanaian institutions were initiated and nurtured under such an atmosphere. Secondly, the volume of investment and the foreign exchange required to import the necessary inputs exerted strain on the balance of payments position of the economy and set in motion a spiral of economic problems that have since then characterized the social and economic environment in Ghana.

Fortunately, much has changed for the better since 1985. Through a combination of several factors, including a structural adjustment programme financed with credit facilities from IMF and the World Bank, the will of individual Ghanaians to survive, and sheer luck (in the form of the return of the rains), the worst of the disasters had been put away by 1986. Efforts at restructuring the economy and remedying the negative policies of past governments have helped to put the economy back on its keel. These macro-economic improvements have, however, not brought manifest improvements in the economic lives of the majority of Ghanaians.

The economy was pulled back from the brink of collapse. The annual rate of inflation has declined to an average of 30% and GDP growth rate has averaged 5% between 1986 and 1996 — an impressive achievement by African standards.

These macro-economic achievements have, however, not been translated to economic well-being for many Ghanaians. Household expenditure in the urban area is four times the minimum wage, thereby providing moral legitimacy for the widespread corruption in public institutions in particular. What is more, the income distribution still discriminates against the rural people where the annual income of most people is far below the national average of $450.

The Rawlings government, however, still has high ambitions, hoping to make Ghana a middle income country by the year 2020. The private sector is expected to be the engine of growth in the coming years, leaving the government to devote its energy and resources to providing infrastructure, social welfare and good governance.

# CHAPTER 5

# Religions and Customs

It is often said that religious considerations dominate the ordering of daily life in African societies. This statement certainly holds true for Ghana. Ghanaians are generally religious and their shared religious beliefs constitute the fundamental basis of their sense of social identity, values and destiny.

Ghana has her share of external religious influences. In the pre-colonial period, Islam gained a foothold in the north, due to contacts with Arabian traders. Even today, the largest proportion of Ghanaian Muslims live in the north. Later on when the Christian missionaries arrived, they concentrated their work on the coastal areas which were the centres of early European trade. Their penetration of the north was, however, impeded by a host of problems including transport difficulties and the established position of Islam in the area.

According to a census in 1960, 42.8% of the Ghanaian population that year were Christians, 38.2% believed in what is normally referred to as traditional gods, 12% were Muslims, and 7% belonged to other religions. It seems that there has not been a significant departure from this pattern in recent years.

The impact of foreign religious influences, although substantial, has not been as pronounced in Ghana as in other parts of the world. Traditional religious beliefs and practices still govern the lives of a majority of the people. An understanding of Ghanaian culture is therefore impossible without an insight into these traditional beliefs and their customary demands. This chapter therefore focuses mainly on describing the philosophical thoughts that guide these religious practices.

It needs to be stressed from the outset that when we talk

about beliefs, the question of truthfulness or falsity does not arise. Some of the views presented here may sound plain wrong to some readers. Nevertheless they constitute fundamental elements of Ghanaian life and must be respected for that reason.

SPIRITS AND THEIR ROLES IN LIFE

The traditional belief is that all entities on earth (both living and non-living) possess life. Rivers, stones and thunder are as much alive as human beings, trees and animals — they are all different manifestations of life. Life is composed of two elements — spirit and matter. Spirits are normally fleshless and therefore not visible to the ordinary eyes. But because of their high powers, they are capable of inhabiting natural objects of their choice. Trees, rocks and rivers can therefore become dwelling places for spirits. Contrary to popular misconception, the physical objects themselves are not the objects of worship and veneration in Ghanaian traditional religion; it is rather the spirits which inhabit them that are venerated or worshipped.

The distinction between spirits and their physical habitation does not, however, come out clearly in everyday speech and this may give rise to misunderstanding. The spirits are usually called by the name of the object in which they dwell. Lake Bosomtwi, for example, is believed to be the dwelling place of the deity called Bosomtwi. There is a hierarchy in the world of spirits. At the apex is God, the Suprem  Being who, for various reasons, has chosen not to live close   1uman beings. Because of the distance between God and m.  , He has sent down earthly gods to function as His deputies.

# Earthly Gods

The earthly gods are believed to be geographically and functionally decentralized. Each community and village has its own god(s); even some households and individuals have their own gods. The power of a god is measured by the number of villages in which its influence has been observed. Thus a community god is believed to be superior to a village god and the latter superior to lineage or clan gods.

The specialized functions of the gods relate to the specific needs of the community, hence the existence of several gods in a given community. The Ewe, for example, believe that *So* (thunder) is a sky god and functions as the Supreme Being's executioner. God's dissatisfaction with the Ewe is communicated to them through *So*. It uses lightning, excessive rainfall or drought as its medium of communication. This invariably results in loss of lives and property. God's creative deputy is called *Se* (which means order, law and harmony). Similarly, there are various gods of harvest, war, hunting, etc.

Due to their functions, these spirits are in continuous contact with human beings and exert immense influence on their daily life. Their overriding purpose is to help people to live in harmony with nature, the spiritual world in general, and with each other. To live in this three-fold harmony, the limited human mind must be guided by the divine wisdom of the gods. Consequently, earthly gods sanction the rules of harmony and give people early warning signals when the rules are violated. As mentioned earlier, the signals come in such forms as droughts and earthquakes with their destructive consequences. Although these warnings bring about immediate hardships, the gods are not believed to act offensively in these matters. Warnings must be severe enough to induce the desired changes in human behaviour. Once people mend their behaviour and harmony is restored, they continue to enjoy the blessings of the gods. In effect, the relationship between human beings and their earthly gods is basically pragmatic and reciprocal. Ghanaians serve their gods and submit to their guidance; in return they demand protection, peace, happiness and long life as their reward. When requested, the gods can also intervene to set affairs straight among people and redress injustice. They are believed to be impartial in their judgement.

There exist other spirits who operate alongside the earthly gods. This group of spirits usually function through witches, and sorcerers or *juju* men to destroy human lives or impose other forms of hardship on people. The Ghanaian's attitude to spirits can therefore be seen as a mixture of fear and respect. When an unhappy incident or natural catastrophe occurs within a community or a household, the cause could either be a bad spirit with a destructive intention or an earthly god giving a warning signal to the people concerned. Incidents are therefore considered as symptoms, the underlying causes of which require clarification.

Gods have several roles to play. They are still considered by most people as guarantors of their society's ethical and moral codes. They are very strict and impartial in their judgement and are therefore invoked by the weak to intervene on their behalf if their rights are trampled upon. Thus a conflict between two persons can be elevated from personal level to a spiritual and therefore societal level if one of the parties to the conflict swears a specific oath and requests a specific god to intervene and punish the other party. The gods are also required to play an investigatory role — for example, in a case of burglary, when the thief is not known.

**Traditional Priests or Diviners**

The task of interpreting the causes of these incidents is the secret lore of a specialized group called diviners who constitute the priesthood of the gods. Each of them is chosen by the gods themselves and undergoes a period of intensive training under a more experienced priest of the same god. The "call" to priesthood occurs in a semi-mystical way: a person suddenly falls ill or behaves in an unusual manner (e.g. goes into a trance). His or her relatives consult a qualified diviner from whom they get to know about the particular god who has decided to "marry" the person. If the relatives fail to do the consultation, the god may reveal itself to the diviner and require him/her to contact the family of the sick person. The sickness may continue until the relatives agree to perform the rites required for the person to commence the training. The training period is usually between six months and three years after which the new priest erects a shrine for the god and begins to practise.

Despite the social status and respect accorded diviners, the influence of Christianity and the numerous personal restrictions as well as financial difficulties involved make people reluctant to join the priesthood. There are, for example, restrictions on the types of food diviners should eat, how they should dress and where they can go.

## The Human Spirit and Destiny

As pointed out earlier, Ghanaians believe that all objects on earth have life which is composed of both matter and spirit. The same holds true of human life. The breath of life and the soul of man come from God. They form that little part of the creator inherent in every man and give life to the flesh. When withdrawn, the body dies. God is therefore the giver of life, not man. When alive, the human spirit and body are inseparable.

Disagreement exists, however, on the contributions made by a father and a mother to a child's life. Among the Akan, a mother is believed to give her child its blood (bogya), and the father its spirit (sunsum). God gives the soul (okra) and the breath of life (honhom). The blood transmitted by a mother to her child establishes its social link or lineage. This explains why the Akan inheritance system is matrilineal.

A father's sunsum moulds the child and establishes its ego or distinctive personality. At a metaphysical level, a child is bound to its father through the identicality of their sunsum. The events in one's life — fortunes and misfortunes, sufferings and joys — are the results of one's destiny and actions. As mentioned earlier, an individual's actions may offend the ancestral spirits and community gods and the offender may be punished accordingly. The origin and effects of one's destiny are, however, difficult to establish.

The general belief is that a person's destiny is determined by God. Destiny is received alongside the breath of life. In addition to issuing individual destinies, God also determines the collective destiny of a household, a clan or even an entire community. People are born into families in which their destinies fit them and as a result they share the collective destiny of those families. It follows therefore that destiny establishes a framework for human behaviour. Some people are destined to be kind, hardworking and obedient while others are destined to be the opposite.

## The Relationship Between the Living and the Dead

The view that Africans worship their dead relatives is widespread among Westerners. It is therefore purposeful to explain the relationship between the living and the dead in Ghana in greater detail. A good starting point is the Ghanaian view of death. Ghanaians believe in the eternity of life. That is, life continues after biological death. At death, the God-given spirit departs in its fleshless form and starts its journey back to the world of spirits, where it remains. However, it maintains contact with the living and continues to mediate between the spiritual world and the world of the living when conflicts between these two worlds arise. It is in this respect that death is described as an invisible cord which links people to their ancestors.

Death is, however, not accepted as good. It brings about uncomfortable disruptions in the socio-economic environment of the living. Ghanaian funeral songs draw attention to death's negative consequences. But as the bereaved family mourns their loss, they find some comfort in the thought that the newly dead person will carry messages to the earlier departed ancestors about their needs and problems. And having just left the problems, the dead person will be motivated to use his/her heightened spiritual powers to protect the living relatives.

Death does not automatically qualify a spirit to become an ancestral spirit. A person must satisfy some special conditions while alive for his/her spirit to be recognized and accorded respect after death. The dead person must, for example, be "an adult". Adulthood in Ghana is not necessarily determined by age, but by having a child. A boy or a girl of 15 is considered an adult if he or she has a child, while childless bachelors or spinsters are considered immature. The reason is simply that by remaining unmarried, the person deliberately refuses to contribute to the continuity of the lineage. His/her spirit is therefore not worth remembering. However, the spirit of childless married couples qualify, especially if they have contributed to the continuity of the lineage by helping raise the children of their relatives.

It is worth mentioning at this point that Ghanaians do not look negatively at having children outside marriage. Although there is a deep respect for marriage as a social institution (see Chapter 6) it is socially and spiritually better to have a child outside marriage than to die childless.

The cause of death is also an important consideration. A tragic death through accident is considered "unclean". As noted earlier, such a death may be due to gross and persistent violations of the sanctions of the gods and the ancestors. As a way of discouraging the occurrence of fatal accidents, these people are not mentioned by name when libations are poured to ancestors in general. In the same vein suicides are viewed seriously. A suicide is a disgrace to the dead person and his/her clan. The corpse is not given a befitting burial and rites are performed to remove "whatever curse had forced the person to commit suicide". In this way the Ghanaian culture attempts to discourage people from taking their own lives.

## The Protective Functions of Ancestors

As in the case of the earthly gods, the relationship between Ghanaians and their ancestors is pragmatic. The ancestors are venerated and rituals are performed to ensure their link with the earthly life from which they departed. In return they protect their descendants against misfortunes such as accidents and premature death. The ancestors withdraw their protection and blessings when they are neglected, thereby placing their descendants at the mercy of their enemies.

The ancestors are also believed to be guardians of the moral codes of the Ghanaian society. They punish their descendants for any breach, either by omission or commission, of any of the established moral principles of the clan. But aggrieved ancestors seldom kill their descendants. It is perhaps worth mentioning that ancestors have no supernatural powers in their own right; whatever influence they exert on earthly life is derived from the Supreme Being.

## Communion with Ancestral Spirits

Ancestors may communicate with their descendants in many different ways. But the most popular of them is through dreams. Ancestral spirit appears in dreams only when an important message is to be delivered to the living as promptly as possible. The spirit may either scold the family head for a neglect which could bring havoc to the family or warn him against an imminent danger. It may then offer direct guidance as the situation requires. Persistent misfortunes suffered by members of a household can also be a sign of ancestral displeasure and must be regarded as a warning to the descendants. When in doubt the people concerned consult diviners for clarification of what might be wrong.

SPIRITUAL AND CUSTOMARY PRACTICES

## Witchcraft

Witchcraft is not a unique Ghanaian phenomenon. But its impact on people's way of thinking and behaviour is perhaps stronger here than in many other parts of the world. For this reason many visitors may not be familiar with its social and psychological implications. It is therefore appropriate to draw the reader's attention to what Ghanaians understand by witchcraft and its mode of operation. It is, however, important to remind ourselves that the discussion here is not concerned with the truthfulness or falsity of the ideas presented.

Witchcraft is believed to be a spiritual power which can inhabit almost any object. The object could be a ring, a string of beads, a talisman, a piece of cloth or any other object usable to human beings. There are also weird instances of witchcraft believed to be inherent in a lump on the body or a fibroid in the tummy or even a snake living within the human body. Both sexes can be witches although women are widely believed to be the most common agents. (This belief is consistent with the general belief that women are more vulnerable to the influence of spirits).

Some people are born witches. That is, they inherit the witchcraft object before their birth. Others inherit theirs from their close relatives. Usually a dying witch is believed to transfer the witchcraft to a beloved descendant, but without the knowledge and consent of the inheritor. (Among the Asante, it is believed that a person can bewitch another only if the two belong to the same matrilineage). There are many other mediums of transmission, including food, drinks or gifts.

Witchcraft is a bad spirit. For this reason witches are accused of many of the misfortunes in Ghanaian families, especially when more logical explanations cannot be found. They are believed to be capable of killing their victims by mystical means. The victim's blood is sucked gradually over several months or even years until the person finally dies. Thus nearly all protracted illnesses are believed to be inflicted by witches who are also believed to inflict poverty, accidents, barenness and even crop failures. They are believed to make invisible perforations in a victim's palm or pocket, making the person's money vanish mysteriously. They make trees fall on people or even overturn vehicles in which they travel.

## Juju

Individuals can of their own choice solicit the mystical powers inherent in nature to fulfil their personal interest. The exercise of such powers is popularly called *juju* and those who apply them are called *juju men*. It must be noted that while diviners are chosen by the gods and enjoy great respect in their communities, juju men are feared for their powers but are not accorded much respect due to their destructive tendencies.

There is juju for almost every human activity; for example, winning the love of a beautiful girl, winning a football match or protecting people against dangers of any kind. Juju men are hired by other people to perform these and many other services. Many stories are told about the protective powers of juju men. A popular story among the Ewe goes like this: In one of the inter-tribal wars fought many years ago, six juju men were chosen to guard the king's palace. None of them had any weapon but were armed with charms and amulets. Deep in the night while the soldiers were engaged in a fight several kilometres away, a band of thirty strong men from the enemy camp sneaked into the village to capture the king. On seeing them three of the juju men dashed forward to meet them with their palms outstretched while chanting *Da male! Da male!* literally meaning "Shoot, and I'll catch! Shoot, and I'll catch!" The enemies fired their guns and the juju men caught the bullets in their open palms. Terrified, the soldiers fled into the bush, some dropping their guns during the flight. This was a real bravery and a demonstration of the powers of juju!

## Medicinemen

The term medicineman or herbalist is commonly used to describe all people who use a combination of herbal and spiritual curatives to restore the health of patients. Diviners as well as juju men can function as medicinemen. Despite the increasing development in medical facilities and general education, most Ghanaians still place their hope and trust in the curative powers of traditional healers. The reason can be found in the central position that spirits hold in the lives of many people. Most protracted illnesses are believed to have spiritual causes. It is only when the gods have withdrawn their blessings that people can fall victim to a serious illness. A complete cure is impossible until the underlying spiritual disturbance is removed.

Through their link with the spiritual world, the medicineman can make a total diagnosis — both biological and spiritual. Two people may suffer from illnesses with the same biological causes. But to a Ghanaian the illnesses are not the same. Each patient's case must be seen as special. It is only when the medicineman provides a complete explanation of the reasons for the illness that the patient's anxiety diminishes and a cure becomes effective.

Let us take a simple example. A snake enters a room and bites a person. A Westerner may explain this event as a mere accident. This explanation will hardly satisfy most Ghanaians. The victim may want to know why the snake chooses to *enter that particular* house and not any of the others in the village; and why it enters *that particular* room at *that particular* time. A mystical explanation is much more appealing, especially when that type of snake is known to avoid human surroundings.

The medicineman's role under such situations is very clear. He understands his patient's socio-cultural and religious demands and can therefore provide a more comprehensive and satisfying diagnosis. His diagnosis (and cure) no doubt has a significant psychological value. It helps to restore not only the biological balance of the patient but his/her spiritual balance as well.

Every medicineman has a special way of effecting a cure. No general description of the procedure is therefore possible. But most spiritual cures require some form of ritual (described later) and the use of herbs, amulets and charms which are believed to contain mystical powers.

Medicinemen have many other important functions in the society. They are important members of the councils of elders in the villages, advising chiefs on issues relating to the spiritual welfare of the community. They observe changes in the natural environment, pray to the gods for their guidance and protection. They are also called upon to perform ceremonies that link the spiritual world with the world of the living. Thus all ceremonies marking major transitions in human lives (e.g. outdooring, marriage and burials) require the presence of diviners.

## Rituals

The most visible form of traditional worship is the ritual performed to acknowledge the presence of the earthly gods and ancestral spirits and to communicate with them. There are rites for nearly every aspect of human life and behaviour because the spiritual world must be continually informed about changes in individual lives and the human society at large. The rites vary in their complexity depending on the occasion or reasons for which they are performed. But the most common features include the pouring of libation and animal offerings. The traditional priests (diviners) feature prominently in ritual performances at the village and community levels. At the household or clan level, the head of the household or a person designated by custom for such duties may be in charge of the rituals. As usual, local practices vary widely in their details, but a few commonalities can be noted. It is, for example, a custom for Ghanaians to pour a bit of whatever they are about to drink on the floor before they put their lips to it. By this gesture, they symbolically share the drink with their ancestors. Naturally, the ancestors must drink first. The drink is poured on the ground because the ancestral spirits are believed to live underground. The earth is therefore the intimate point of contact between the living and their ancestors.

Traditional prayers are also conducted with drinks. This practice recognizes the Ghanaian custom that one does not go to a respectable person empty-handed. To show one's respect to the person, a gift (usually a drink) must be taken along. Similarly, one cannot address the spirits without first giving them something to drink. The type of drink used for a prayer depends on the nature of the ceremony. On some occasions, local gin or palm wine is used while other ceremonies require schnapps. The ritual usually starts with the officiant (always a man) taking off his shoes (as a sign of respect for the spirits) and asking for silence from those gathered. He holds the calabash or glass with two hands and pours a bit of the drink on the floor while calling the spirits and ancestors by their names and inviting them to drink. He then tells them the purpose of the invitation and the requests from those gathered. He always remembers to ask for good health and prosperity for every individual in the household and/or community. It is recognized that not every spirit drinks alcohol. For this reason the prayer ends with the officiant offering water to those spirits who drink only water. After the prayer the officiant is served with the drink first in appreciation of his service. It is only then that the rest of the participants at the ceremony are served with drinks.

## Animal Offering

Since spirits are in close and regular contact with people, they are believed to eat the same food as human beings. This is why food may be placed in the shrines of earthly gods and ancestors or even on the graves of newly departed relatives. Sacrifice of animals such as cocks, sheep, goats or cows have additional significance in Ghanaian customs. They are offered either as tokens of gratitude for the protection and guidance of the spirits or as appeasement for offences committed by individuals. Animal offering is, for example, made on behalf of the whole community during festivals (see Chapter 8) or by individuals when they can afford it. When customary rules are violated, the offender provides the offerings as part of his/her punishment. The type of offering is determined by the gravity of the offence.

# CHAPTER 6

# Institutions and Transitions in Life

The previous chapter has described the spiritual realm of life in Ghana. This chapter takes the reader through life in the mundane world, the cultural context within which the major transitions in life are observed and the link between the living and the spirits as reflected in various symbols and rituals. The aim is to prepare the non-Ghanaian reader to make meaning of these ceremonies if he happens to be invited to any of them.

## Birth and Outdooring Ceremonies

The most natural starting point for the description of Ghanaian social institutions is the birth of a new child. As mentioned earlier, children are the greatest treasure of a Ghanaian. No amount of material wealth can measure up against the satisfaction of having a child. For a man, a child manifests his manhood and establishes him as a respectable and responsible person among his colleagues. Similarly, a woman's greatest pride is her children. They constitute the best security for her marriage since barrenness is a substantial ground for divorce.

It is the belief that the spirit of parents are reproduced in their children. To a Ghanaian, a person may be biologically dead but as long as he has a child alive, he is not "really dead". Children, through libation and propitiation, keep active their dead parents' spiritual relationship with earthly life. In other words, children are necessary to maintain the "immortality" of their parents. The more children one has, the more secure one's "immortality". For the community as a whole, a new child is an additional guarantee that a lineage can continue into the distant future. Prolific child bearing is therefore honoured; parents of large families and mothers of twins and triplets are held in special esteem. (Ghanaians' attitude to twins is quite unique compared to other African societies such as parts of Nigeria and Congo where twins are believed to bring bad luck to their parents. In some of these societies, one of the twins may be secretly killed by the mother at birth in order to avoid the curse of the spirits).

Naturally, pregnancy is the most joyous news in a Ghanaian village. Pregnant women receive exceptional attention from their husbands and family members. Their household chores are reduced, they are discouraged from carrying heavy loads and they eat better food than other members of the household. They are also believed to be more vulnerable to evil forces and require special spiritual protection. Special herbs are prepared for them to strengthen them physically and spiritually, and to ensure "a good labour". When a woman has the unfortunate experience of several miscarriages or her children have been dying successively at birth, the services of special medicinemen are required to protect her pregnancy. When the child is born, it may be given a special name and charms, fixed around its neck for several years in order to get rid of evil spirits that may want to kill it. A child's birth is greeted with two important ceremonies — naming and outdooring ceremonies. Both can be performed on the same day or, as has frequently become the case, on separate days.

**The Naming Ceremony**

The naming ceremony is usually held on the eighth day of the birth. That is, the day the baby is officially proclaimed a member of the family. During the first seven days of its life, a baby is considered to be on a "visit" and undergoing a transition from the world of spirits to earthly life. If it dies during this period, its departure is not supposed to be gravely felt by the parents.

In other words, they are not supposed to show any outward sign of grief. (The possible explanation for this tradition is the high infant mortality rate in Ghana until a few decades ago. Parents were therefore assumed incapable of intervening when a baby decided to return to its origin during the first seven days.) The baby is normally kept indoors and people outside the family are not allowed to see it.

On the eighth day, the baby is believed to agree to stay and must therefore be accorded a formal welcome. In most communities, the ceremony is performed by a person born on the same day of the week as the baby. It takes place during dawn with the morning sun symbolically welcoming the new member of the family when it rises. The ceremony itself proceeds as follows: The baby is laid on a mat in front of the group of family elders who are gathered for the occasion. The family head or diviner says a thanksgiving prayer to God, the ancestors and the protective spirits for their vigilance during the pregnancy and delivery. He then announces the acceptance of the baby as part of the family and commits it again into the protective hands of the spirits. The spirits and ancestors are also called upon to protect the parents, to give them good health and fortune to raise the baby and all subsequent ones.

The person to perform the rituals (i.e. anyone in the family having the same natal day as the baby) calls the baby's name and says: "This is your name. From today you must respond to this name." He/she then touches the child's tongue with a drop of local wine and says: "When you see wine call it wine." The ritual is repeated with water and the words: "When you see water call it water." (Details of the ritual vary from one community to the other.) This ritual has an important symbolic meaning. It is the child's first "lesson" from the human society into which it has just entered. The message is simple: Let the truth be your guide and tell the truth under all circumstances; water must always remain water and wine always wine.

## Outdooring

People outside the family are permitted to see the child only
after the naming ceremony has been performed and, as mentioned earlier, the public appearance can take the form of an
elaborate outdooring ceremony. Due to the financial expenses
involved, outdooring ceremonies in the towns and cities have
become symbols of wealth and social status. In the villages less
elaborate arrangements are preferred. A typical outdooring
ceremony in the cities requires a great deal of preparation. When
the parents of the child are fully prepared, they decide on the
date on which most of their relatives and friends are free from
work and other commitments (e.g. a Sunday) as the day of the
ceremony. Invitations are sent out and practical arrangements
for the occasion start: A band may be hired to play on the
occasion, drinks and food are bought, etc. On the day of the
ceremony, the baby and its parents wear white clothes as a sign
of joy. The invited guests come with various forms of presents,
including money to the baby and its mother. Food and drinks
are served while the orchestra plays popular dance music. As
the party progresses, the names of those who offered gifts are
announced to the gathering and they are greeted with cheers.
The party usually starts in the afternoon and may continue deep
into the night.

## Ghanaian Names

Naming of children in Ghana reveals a number of fundamental
social attitudes and cultural practices. The child is by right entitled
to at least three names. The first is given according to the particular
day of the week on which it is born. A male child born on a
Friday is called Kofi, and a female Afua or some other variations
of these. Saturday males are named Kwame and females Ama.
These natal day names (See the accompanying table) are some-

times referred to as God's names, implying that God decrees the day on which people are born.

## GHANAIAN NATAL DAY NAMES

| Day | Male | Female |
|-----|------|--------|
| Sunday (Kwasida) | Kwesi/Kwasi | Akosua |
| Monday (Dzoda) | Kwadzo/Kudjo | Adzo/Adjoa |
| Tuesday (Blada) | Kwabena/Kwabla | Abla/Abena |
| Wednesday (Kuda) | Kwaku/Kweku | Akua/Aku |
| Thursday (Yawoda) | Yawo/Yaw | Yawa/Yaa |
| Friday (Fida) | Kofi | Afi/Afua |
| Saturday (Memleda) | Kwame | Ama/Ami |

The second is the so-called patronymic names chosen by the parents. This can be the name of any member of the family (living or dead) whom the child's parents wish to honour. By giving the baby that person's name, the parents hope that the baby will be inspired by the name to follow the footsteps of that person as it grows into an adult. The third name is the family name or surname which is usually the name of the child's grandfather. A father and a son may therefore have different surnames. A baby may also be given other names according to the order of position in which it comes among its brothers and sisters and/or the circumstances under which it is born. The third of three consecutive male children is called Mensah and his female counterpart is called Mansah. Twins also have special names in every ethnic group. The same holds true for a child born immediately after twins. Ghanaian families with

European ancestors have also retained their "foreign" surnames, for example Reindorf, Hansen, Wood and Fynn.

## Christening of Children

One obvious influence of Christianity on Ghanaian culture is the so-called Christian names which are given by Christian parents to their children when they are baptized, just as in the Western countries. As a result, many first names in Ghana are Christian names like John, James and Jane. In recent years, local names have been accepted by the churches as Christian names. Among the Ewe, such names as Akofa and Dzigbodi have now replaced their English versions of Comfort and Patience, and other names without English equivalents (for example Senyo, Enyonam and Edem) have also become popular Christian names.

### TRANSITION FROM INFANCY TO ADULTHOOD

A child's growth is closely watched by both its parents and the entire community. As a rule, boys drift towards their father, uncles and the men in the community. Among these adults, they are taught the role men play in the family and community. Similarly, the girls drift towards their mother and aunts under whose keen supervision they receive their training to become responsible women of the community. Upbringing of children is therefore a community responsibility. In other words, every adult has a duty to guide the younger members of the community. Consequently, every man and woman in the extended family about the age of the child's father and mother is recognized by the child as its "parent".

The transition to adulthood is therefore celebrated as a community affair. An elaborate ritual is usually performed to demonstrate the family's (and the entire community's) joy and gratitude to their ancestors and gods for protecting their child and guiding it during its youthful days. Among some communities any youth who did not go through such a ceremony was considered not a complete person.

## Puberty (or Nubility) Rites Among the Asante

The most detailed published study of nubility rites in Ghana is among the Asante. Apart from minor local differences, this study can be taken to reflect the general pattern in Ghana as a whole.

A girl's transition to adulthood is seen first in her physical development, particularly her breasts. Girls (as well as their mothers) watch the development of their breasts with great interest and discuss their physical development among themselves with obvious joy and excitement about their approaching womanhood. Some Asante girls even apply concoctions to their breasts to accelerate their growth and to enable them take their proper and admirable shape. Many adolescent girls feel shy to expose their growing breasts, but a few of them leave them uncovered. The intention is not to tease the males or to indicate their sexual maturity. It merely indicates how naturally they feel about their physical development.

A young woman is not considered to reach full womanhood before her first menstrual experience. Her first menstruation is therefore celebrated as a significant event in her life. After this she becomes eligible to be considered for her nubility rites.

The procedure begins with the young woman's mother informing the queen mother of the community of her daughter's readiness to be initiated. About a century ago, the worst disgrace a young woman could bring upon her family was to be pregnant before her nubility rites. Young women were therefore discouraged from having sexual experience before these rites had been performed. In order to ensure that the young woman was not pregnant at the time of the ceremony, the queen mother had to examine her during three consecutive menstrual periods. When fully satisfied with her examinations, a date was set for the ceremony. But all these restrictions have been removed in present day Ghana and attitude to sex has become more relaxed. Today the queen mother gives her consent without these elaborate controls. The ceremony itself has both religious and social dimensions. The Asante believe that nubility rites are ordained by their ancestors. To ignore them is to slight the ancestors. There are therefore only very rare instances where a young woman is exempted from these rites. Even in these cases, diviners are consulted to seek the spirits' consent for the exemption.

## Ritual for Young Men

The initiation ceremonies for young men are less elaborate and differ widely from one locality to the other. Boys are expected to be brave and capable of protecting their households and communities against attacks from wild animals and enemies. Bravery must be demonstrated both as an individual and as part of a team.

In some communities, a young boy experiences his first test of bravery through circumcision. The operation, which involves removing the foreskin of the boy's penis, is performed by a skilled medicineman or herbalist after a short ceremony. The blood shed by the boy through circumcision symbolizes his preparedness to shed his blood as a man if called upon by circumstances to do so in the future. When he grows into a young man his father gives him a symbolically important gift — a gun or any other kind of weapon used in the community. The presentation is preceded by a short ceremony at which the elders of the clan are present. At this ceremony, prayers are offered to the gods asking for their protection and guidance in periods of danger.

This ceremonial gift of weapon is no longer fashionable in most parts of Ghana. But young men still have opportunities to demonstrate their bravery, particularly in groups during festivals. On these occasions, they dress in traditional battle clothes such as raffia skirts and *batakari*, using amulets, horns and hides of wild animals as decorations. They sing war songs while dancing or marching through the principal streets, reminding the audience of the gallantry and military victories of their forefathers.

The three-hundred-year old deer hunting festival among the Effutu of Winneba in central Ghana is one of the few occasions on which young men still taste the spirit of bravery in the traditional style. According to this tradition, a live deer must be sacrificed to the community god annually, and this sacrificial animal must be caught by hand in the forest. The young men in the community are divided into two groups called *asafo groups* and they compete with each other for the credit of being the first to present the sacrificial deer on the day declared for the ceremony. The preparations for the competition include rites, planning, organizing into smaller sub-groups and rehearsing the expedition with military precision. The traditional priests and juju men usually play an active role. Old charms are activated and the assistance of new ones sought.

On the day of the expedition, the two groups dress in military outfit, armed with sticks and cudgels. They enter the forest by cock-crow and the group that succeeds in catching the first deer runs back home with shouts of victory, carrying the animal shoulder high through the streets to the centre of the crowd gathered for the occasion. The rest of the ceremony involves slaughtering the animal amidst merry-making in which the whole community participates.

## MARRIAGE

Marriage is an old and respectable social institution the world over. Every society has evolved rules and procedures to govern it, separating the permissible from the forbidden in the relationship. These rules and practices form an essential and integral part of the society's culture. The same is true in Ghana. Marriage in Ghana is more than a private relationship between a man and a woman. It is a major transition point in the lives of young people; and their relatives take a keen interest in it. Through it the torch of life is transferred from one generation to another. The descendants join the already large group of relatives, bringing additional glory or shame to it. Marriage therefore unites families and clans. It may even mark the beginning of a new lineage or community. Consequently, the decision to get married is considered too important to be left completely to the two parties involved, especially when they are young and inexperienced. The elders must guide them and the ancestors' blessings must be sought.

There are three types of marriage in Ghana. These are: (i) customary marriage, (ii) statutory marriage (i.e. marriage under ordinance and other statutes), and (iii) church marriage (both Christian and Muslim). Statutory marriage is of a comparatively recent origin and is confined mainly to educated young people in towns and cities. Since customary marriage is still the most predominant form of marriage, we shall devote the rest of this section to a detailed description of the process.

## Choosing a Marriage Partner in the Customary Way

It hardly needs pointing out that marriage in Ghana is sanctioned only between opposite sexes. What is less known is that women play a vigorous role in bringing it about. The first step naturally is to find a partner. A fairly widespread practice is for a young man to take the initiative to find a woman of his choice and inform his parents about it. But there also exists the practice of parents matching their children without their prior knowledge. The informal contacts and shuttles between the two families are usually the tasks of women.

A young man's mother may approach the mother of a young

woman and casually suggest the possibility of their children marrying each other. A mother would take such an initiative to ensure that her daughter-in-law, in her judgement, would make a good wife for her son. A mother to a young woman may have the same wishes, i.e. looking for a suitable man for her beloved daughter. The parents then inform their children about their plans, impressing on them that their choice is in their best interest. In nearly all cases the children accept the judgement of their mothers. Occasionally, however, a young woman may not consider the choice acceptable. Under such a situation, her aunts join her mother to woo her. This may take several weeks or months. When the daughter proves unyielding to her parents' wishes, other elders of the family may be invited to talk to her.

In the more common situation where a young man makes his own choice, beauty may be his first and foremost criterion for the woman he chooses. Women with rounded cheeks graced with smile and who are generously endowed with bosom and buttocks stand a better chance. Other details include the skin complexion and the shape of her calf. Those who are relatively fairer in complexion and whose calves are fleshy gain extra advantage. But parents look at other attributes too. Once a son has informed his mother of his interest in a particular woman, the mother will undertake an investigation into the young woman's family background. The investigation is to ascertain both the physical and spiritual conditions of her family. Evidence of chronic ill health or frequent accidents in the family would make the woman a less welcome choice. The woman's family undertakes similar investigations into the man's family background. Satisfactory results from these enquiries open up the way for the second phase.

A delegation of elders from the man's family is then sent to the woman's family to formally ask for her hand in marriage. A reply is usually not given on this first visit. The visit is repeated once or twice before the woman's parents give their consent. The hesitation has a symbolic significance. It is to emphasize the importance attached to marriage. A woman is too precious to her parents for them to part with her so readily. If the man really wants her, he should be prepared to wait for a while. Meanwhile the prospective couple can start visiting each other openly. It is usually the man who does the visiting. A few decades ago the man could visit the woman only at her parent's house. Meeting privately was discouraged between them in order to avoid the temptation of sexual relations before the marriage. Premarital sexual relations are now treated with great tolerance and these restrictions are no longer valid. When the prospective couple live far from each other, the visits are usually less frequent. They may see each other on only a few occasions (or never at all) prior to the marriage ceremony.

**Marriage Gifts**

It is a common practice for the bride's parents to receive some items from the groom as part of the marriage ceremony. These items vary according to local customs. They may include some amount of money, cow(s), tobacco and drinks.The relatively high economic value of some of these items has led to a general misinterpretation of the purposes for which they are offered. They have been erroneously called "bride price" or "bride-wealth", thereby giving the impression that women in Ghana (and other parts of Africa) are sold into marriage.

Other interpretations see these items as "compensations" for the labour the woman's parents will lose when she leaves home to join her husband. Such perceptions are alien to the Ghanaian concept of marriage. The items are given as a token of gratitude, an appreciation for the opportunity to marry a woman who is cherished so much by her parents. They are certainly not a measure of the woman's value in any respect. This symbol of respect and gratitude constitutes the formal seal on the marriage and accords the relationship the status it deserves within the community. Through their offer and acceptance, the two families become united. The man is not only reminded that the woman has a family which cares very much for her, but he is also offered an open arm, a hearty welcome into that family as long as he takes good care of the woman, the same way her parents would.

Failure to marry a woman in a proper customary manner is a disgrace to both the man and the wife. The woman is always reminded by her parents that her husband "is not known" to them. She cannot expect her family's sympathy and assistance if the relationship runs into trouble. In a nutshell, marriage gifts elevate the respect attached to the woman both as a person and a wife. By requiring these gifts, women are discouraged from living with men who do not respect them and their families. Even people who choose religious or statutory marriage ceremony still perform these customs in order to legitimize their marriage in the eyes of the woman's family and ancestors.

### Customary Marriage Ceremony

A date is fixed for the marriage when the man's parents inform the woman's parents that they are ready with the bride gifts. A wedding day is usually a "safe" day, i.e. a day on which the spirits of the locality are at rest and can be "invited" to witness the ceremony and bless the new couple. The ceremony is held at the home of the woman's parents. The families of both parents are required to be present. All the young people in the clan are also invited. The ceremony therefore brings the two clans or households together. Any existing disputes between the families are resolved through arbitration prior to the day of the ceremony.

The ceremony itself is hardly an elaborate affair for the ordinary people. (Rich families, no doubt, indulge in excesses that are meant to demonstrate their social status). It consists essentially of the presentation of the bride gifts by the man's family and their acceptance by the woman's family. Before their acceptance, the woman is asked formally in the presence of everyone if she agrees to the man's proposal to marry her. If her reply is in the affirmative, the woman's parents acknowledge receipt of the gift and both parties exchange thanks. Libation is poured to invite and inform the ancestral spirits and the gods of the community about the happy news and ask them for their continual guidance and blessings. The drinks are then shared among the people gathered. A special quantity of local drinks is given to the young men of the village or locality as a way of announcing to them that the young woman concerned is no longer "free". As the drinking continues, the elders offer advice to the new couple about how to start a new life and what marriage entails.

## Commencement of Married Life

In the strictest sense, the ceremony marks the beginning of the couple's marital life. The woman is now at liberty (or, in some localities, required) to leave her parents' home and live with the man. Again, in its ideal form, Ghanaian culture requires that the man sees the woman's nakedness only after the marriage. Virginity is a symbol of physical, moral and spiritual purity. When a virgin woman joins her husband in bed for the first time she does so with pride and deep satisfaction for her moral uprightness. As mentioned earlier, attitude to sex has, however, been greatly relaxed in recent years. It is no longer a shame to indulge in premarital sex. Nevertheless, the status of virginity has not changed radically. Many men still take pride in marrying a virgin, if they are fortunate to find one.

## Divorce

The greatest wish of every couple is to live together for the rest of their lives. But many do not succeed in their endeavour to make the relationship work. Ghanaian culture allows for divorce, when there is a good reason for it. Childlessness, adultery and quarrelsomeness are some of the common reasons for which couples break their marriage. When a couple begins to encounter difficulties, the parties seek advice from their respective parents. The woman's mother may be invited to stay with them for a month or more, observe their behaviour towards each other and advise her daughter on how to adjust to the situation. She may talk to the man herself or ask other elders in the family to do so. The man's mother may play the same role with the consent of the man's wife.

If the conflict persists, the parties are usually encouraged to settle the disputes at an arbitration during which elders in the families share their experience with them and encourage them to resolve their differences. If realistic settlement is impossible, either of the parties is free to initiate a divorce. He or she informs the spouse's parents about the decision by presenting them with a bottle of schnapps. The parties are called again to a meeting with the elders of both families and if the party demanding the divorce upholds the demand, the elders dissolve the marriage at that meeting. There are no specific rules regarding custody and financial support of children after the divorce. Agreements are usually arrived at between the couple with the assistance of their families. Normally, young children remain living with their mother, but the father still has custody over them until they are married or are of age.

## Polygamy

Societies throughout the world practise two main forms of marriage: (i) monogamy, where a person marries only one spouse, and (ii) polygamy, where a person has several spouses. There are two forms of polygamy: (i) polygyny, practised in societies that allow a man to marry more than one woman, and

(ii) polyandry, found in societies where a woman is allowed to marry more than one man.

In Ghana polygyny is allowed. That is, men can marry more than one wife under customary law. Within the muslim communities, this concession is religiously sanctioned. Some Christian sects forbid it. But even in communities where it is practised, the man is required to seek the permission of his most senior wife before marrying another woman. It must, however, be pointed out that only few men can afford to have more than one wife at a time. Polygyny is therefore considered by many as a luxury. It is more common for Ghanaian men to enter into several marriages but with one woman at a time. Christians who want to enjoy the benefits of polygyny and at the same time uphold their religious privileges, may marry one woman in church (his so-called wedded wife) while marrying the others the customary way.

Polygny is often presented as an interesting example of communal life and interdependence within Ghanaian rural families. When one wife gives birth, the other wife (or wives as the case may be) nurses her and cares for her other children during the time she is regaining her vitality. If one wife dies, others take over the care of her children. In cases of sickness, other wives fetch water, collect firewood, cook and do other household chores. A married woman can visit her parents as frequently as she chooses or as the situation demands. She may stay away for weeks or months without this disturbing her marital relationship. The wives, their children and husband constitute one large family in which interdependence and flexibility are greatly encouraged. There may be misunderstandings between the women but in deed, such misunderstandings are quickly buried and give way to cooperation.

Doubtlessly, such forms of living have negative sides. Some critics maintain that members of the family lose their individual identity and are forced to contribute to the livelihood of others.

The efforts of those who struggle to improve their living conditions can be hindered by the need to share the little they have even before their efforts start to yield substantial results. The economic progress of the individual and the community as a whole may therefore be unnecessarily retarded. This criticism is not wholly true. Ghanaian families do encourage the efforts of promising individuals. Contributions are, for example, made to sponsor the education of children with outstanding school records or to help members in the family start their own business. These contributions are voluntary and the individuals receive them as presents and not loans. The family's only expectation is that the beneficiaries will make appropriate contribution to others' development in the future. In this way everyone enjoys the benefits of this togetherness according to his or her capacity and needs.

## BURIAL AND FUNERAL CEREMONIES

Death closes in on every person with every passing day. As people grow older the tempo of their bodily mechanism slows down. Finally the unavoidable happens; they die either suddenly or after a protracted illness. As mentioned earlier, death marks an individual's final transition in this life, that is to say, from the earthly life to the world of spirits.

Funeral ceremonies in Ghana are primarily meant to adequately prepare the soul for this important journey. They are also considered to be the final measure of a person's achievements in his or her lifetime, and an indication of how the departing soul is going to be received in the spiritual world of its ancestors. The bereaved family therefore makes detailed preparations to give the departed member a befitting goodbye.

The soul begins its journey only after the dead body is buried among the ancestors. For this reason relatives are obliged to convey the corpse of their deceased members from wherever the death occurs back to their ancestral home. However, when a person dies in a foreign country and the cost of conveying the corpse cannot be met by his or her relatives, the deceased person's hair and finger nails must be cut and sent to his or her natal home for burial. It is not only because these parts of the body are easier to transport over long distances but also because they are considered to symbolize important identification features of the dead person in life and in death.

If the person dies at the natal home, clear-cut procedures exist for the burial and funeral ceremonies. The chief of the village is immediately informed about the incident and a meeting of the elders is convened to discuss plans for the burial. Meanwhile, the relatives of the deceased send messages to members of the family who may be living in other parts of the country to come home for the burial and funeral ceremonies. Ghanaians are very cautious in breaking the news of death to their relatives in order to minimize the effects of the shock. Whoever receives the news first tells the others only after they have eaten and are fully relaxed.

**Burial**

Burial usually takes place within twenty-four hours of death in order to avoid the embarrassment of the body decomposing before being buried, due to the humid tropical climate. When the elders have approved the burial plans in consultation with the bereaved family, the chief orders an announcement to be made, officially declaring the person dead and informing the people about the burial plans. Wailing, shouting and singing immediately fill the air, dramatically changing an otherwise quiet village atmosphere. Non-family members join in the wailing, an affirmation of the bonds of social solidarity between the bereaved and other members of the community.

The deceased is washed that evening by a few women in

the family and dressed in white clothes to symbolize the departed soul's joy in joining its ancestors. The dead is then laid in state on a richly decorated bed. Usually a woman sits at the bedside to watch over the body and drive away the flies from it. If the deceased is a Christian, a church service is held during the early part of the evening. Mourners and sympathizers remain after the service to keep wake over the body throughout the night. Tea, coffee, kola nuts and drinks are served by the mourners during the wake-keeping.

The whole community is involved in the practical arrangements for the burial. The men go to the cemetery early in the morning to dig the grave while the women prepare to receive sympathizers who may come from the neighbouring towns and villages for the burial. The coffin is usually provided by the children of the deceased.

Before the body is placed in the coffin, few elders and very close members of the family gather around it to send messages to their ancestors and to perform the final rites that should prepare the departing soul for the journey. Money and other materials may be placed in the coffin beside the body. The understanding is that the soul may need these things on the journey.

A Christian burial is usually preceded by a short church service after which the burial procession is led by the officiating priest to the cemetery for the final part of the ceremony. Deceased persons who belong to the traditional religion are buried according to the ritual prescribed by the gods.

**Funerals**

After the day of the burial, the elders of the village join the bereaved family to plan the funeral. Funeral ceremonies are performed in memory of the deceased as well as mourning the loss to the community. The nature of these ceremonies and their duration vary widely among tribes and localities. But the general considerations include the age of the deceased, his/her status in the community as well as the circumstances surrounding the death. As a rule, dead children are not given any elaborate burial ceremony. Their earthly life is presumed not to have ended and by denying them a good farewell, it is believed that they are motivated to return early to their parents. Very elderly people receive elaborate farewell. This requires the presence of their children and grandchildren and the entire clan. Young and middle-aged people are usually given what may be considered a normal funeral ceremony.

In the past when a chief died, his death was not officially announced until one year later. This practice evolved during the period of slave trade when communities were eager to attack each other at the least opportunity in order to sell the war captives as slaves. It was therefore dangerous for a community to exist (even for a brief period) without a leader. A new chief was therefore installed before the death of his predecessor was made known. The new chief supervised the funeral ceremony of his predecessor. These days the announcement of a chief's death is not kept that long.

Elaborate preparations precede a funeral ceremony. Members of the bereaved family buy dark-brown and/or black cloth to be worn during the funeral (as a symbol of sorrow). A considerable amount of food and drinks are bought to feed and entertain the numerous expected guests. Three days are usually set aside for the ceremony, during which the various customary rites are performed. But the major part of the ceremony is performed on the last day, known to many people as the main funeral day. Sympathizers and friends who wish to offer condolences are expected on that day.

Every member of the bereaved family is busy on the main funeral day. The women prepare meals in large quantities; the men erect sheds, fetch seats and arrange for the purchase of drinks, slaughter the animals to be used in preparing the dishes and so on. The elders sit at home to receive sympathizers who pour in from far and near. As they arrive, they go round shaking hands and exchanging greetings with the mourners. They then announce their funeral donations to the public. The mourners thank them and serve them with drinks. Meanwhile, drumming and dancing are staged in an open space close to the bereaved family's house. Any remaining rituals are performed by the bereaved family; drinks and food are offered to sympathizers from near and afar, contributions to funeral expenses are made by distant relatives friends, etc.

Funerals serve other socially significant purposes. When people are old and know that they are about to die, they arrange to resolve all pending disputes between them and any of their relatives and friends. They must depart with clear conscience in order to secure their continuous contact with the living. If someone dies without resolving the disputes, ceremonies are performed to "bury" whatever misunderstandings that may remain. All funerals are also occasions for big family reunion and all members of the extended family are expected to be present for the ceremonies. Misuderstandings between members of the family are brought before the elders and resolved amicably, marriages may be arranged and family projects planned.

# CHAPTER 7

# Some Underlying Values and Rules of Behaviour

Values and rules of behaviour are defined by the members of every society according to their view of life and history. They are therefore not universal. What may be considered an outrageous conduct in one society may be considered normal, or even praised in another society. Ghanaian values and rules of good behaviour are therefore unique in this respect. In this chapter, the reader is introduced to some of the main values shared across the country and factors currently influencing them. This will hopefully improve visitors' understanding of behaviours they might find strange and in this way encourage the development of good social relations between them and their hosts.

## THE GHANAIAN PERSONALITY

Assimeng (1981, p 76) describes a Ghanaian as being characterized by:

1. Conformity and blatant eschewing of individual speculations
2. Unquestioning acquiescence
3. Lack of self-reliance, owing to the pervading influence of the extended family system
4. Fetish worship of authority and charismatic leaders
5. Hatred of criticism.

With such a personality profile, many Ghanaians will be found to show a strong preference for *the status quo* or be hesitant to alter situations that they found unfavourable, if their actions will involve substantial risk to themselves, their family members and friends. This explains why Ghanaians are easy to govern; and severe abuses of their human rights by governments are scarcely met with public outcry let alone bloody revolt. Even inter-ethnic strife is rare. As Daniel (1993) writes,

> We are law-abiding, brought up to be. There are children who dutifully fetch the cane to be whipped! They grow up to be good Ghanaians. Often during national emergencies especially, announcements come on the air for people to report to the nearest police station to be detained. The good Ghanaian complies. There have been those who had long spells in police cells who should not have been there in the first place, because the invitation to report did not even refer to them by name, only that functionaries of the party dethroned were wanted. There have been others who for answering summons by radio came to untimely death, law-abiding to the end, others who survived though broken in body and spirit — the stories told of happenings behind prison bars, could they all be true?

## THE EXTENDED FAMILY SYSTEM

Family relationships form one of the underlying foundations of a socio-cultural understanding. In many European families, the individual's identity is jealously guarded. His or her behaviour is judged in isolation from the rest of the family. In other words, the association of the members of the family is relatively loose. In many other parts of the world the relationship between the individual and his family is closely knit. The interlocking structure of relationships and obligations found in these societies is referred to as *familism*. As used in sociology, the term describes a form of social organization in which all values are determined by reference to the maintenance, continuity and functioning of the family group. Within such a social framework, all purposes, actions, gains and ideals of individual members are evaluated by comparison with the fortune of the family as a whole. Said differently, one's obligations in life are perceived to begin and end with family groups.

The term *familism* aptly describes the family structures in Ghana. Individual members of the family are bound to one another by the collective moral rules and obligations of the family. The family therefore limits, influences and, in some situations, determines the individual's activities in society. This means, the individual's identity is inextricably linked with the family's. It is a necessary condition for survival in many situations; it decides on the framework of division of labour that ensures livelihood and social advancement for its members and, through that, holds the unit together as an organic whole. The division of labour and distribution of power within the family are determined by age (seniority), the size of financial contribution, genealogical placement and sex. But in recent years the degree of financial contribution has become the overriding consideration.

It is commonly assumed that provided one gets the right type of education and/or some financial resources to begin with, the blessings of social mobility will eventually be enjoyed by the individual; and the family will be relieved of the burden of maintaining that individual's sustenance. It is even hoped that by climbing the social ladder, the individual will help put other members of the family on the first step towards social mobility. Many of the younger generation of African managers excel to the heights of their academic achievements through the collective financial contribution of their extended families and, in some cases, from the whole clan. Since these contributions are seen as investments to yield dividends in folds, it imposes huge social obligations on the beneficiary. In a nutshell, family relations are characterized by individual benefits matched with moral responsibilities. No member of the family who is in genuine need should be denied assistance, no matter what personal miscalculations might have landed him in the hardships. This obligation is usually reinforced by religious sanctions; the ancestral spirits are believed to punish family members that deny others assistance in time of need. Arguably, the material and psychological safety net so provided can generate a sense of complacency in some family members, thereby reducing their contribution to the collective wealth of the family.

## COURTESY

There are many rules of courtesy which a visitor must take note of. But since these rules differ from one locality to another, only a few general ones are presented here. Visitors may supplement the list as they move from one area to the other.

### Verbal Insults

Insulting Ghanaians in the presence of other people is the worst injury one can inflict on their pride. Even a chief cannot insult his subjects in public. It is important to note that words commonly used in Europe and North America in friendly conversations are considered highly insulting if used in Ghana. Examples are "idiot" and "stupid". It is an unpardonable offence for a child or a woman to insult a man with these words, no matter what the cause of the anger might be. Under no circumstance should a child insult an adult of either gender.

### The Use of the Left and the Right Hand

Ghanaians normally use the left hand for filthy things, for example cleaning oneself after toilet visits. For this reason, the left hand is considered unclean. It is therefore an insult to dip one's left hand into food. For the same reason gifts must neither be given nor received with the left hand. When shaking hands with a group of people, traditional courtesy requires that you start with the person on the right. Starting from the left is a grievous insult.

## Greetings

Exchange of greetings is an extremely important social activity. People judge others' attitude to them by the manner in which they greet or respond to greetings. It is not enough to say "hi" to a close friend, a neighbour or a workmate. People who know each other quite well are expected to take some time off their busy daily schedules to greet each other in a warm and affectionate manner. In the villages, family heads get up early in the morning to visit the homes of their relatives to greet them and ask about their health before they start the day's work. If they are hindered from doing so in the morning, they must remember to do it in the evening.

The rules of greeting differ from place to place. It is therefore advisable to enquire about these rules from the citizens of the locality in which you find yourself. But the formal procedure is as follows: The person who is being visited says "Welcome". The visitor says "Thank you". He or she is offered a seat and water to drink. (Water is, however, not offered to a friend on a routine visit unless he/she asks for some). Receiving the water offered by one's host indicates that one has no ill feelings. It is therefore a custom to receive the water even if one is not thirsty, take a mouthful and give the rest back. After drinking the water the visitor greets the host and others in the house. The greetings are normally preceded by hand-shakes. The visitor will get up and shake hands with those gathered, starting from the right. The host will normally ask about the visitor's health and the health of all the others in his/her family.

After the greetings the host enquires about the purpose of the visit. It is then that any serious matter can be discussed. This protocol is usually broken when two friends meet on the street or elsewhere. But it is a good idea for a visitor to learn the formal procedure, especially if one expects to be presented to a group of elders in the village where the protocol is still strictly adhered to.

## Gifts

Westerners frequently remark that Africans are always greatly overjoyed when presented with gifts of relatively little value. They tend to think that this expression of joy is due to the fact that the recipients of these gifts are poor. This is a gross misunderstanding of African culture, and an impartial and observant visitor to Ghana will readily discover this error. Ghanaians cherish giving and receiving presents, irrespective of their monetary value. Gifts are considered as a token of friendship and symbolize goodwill. For this reason people who work outside their natal homes always bring small gifts to members of their family when they visit them. To reject a gift without any significant reason may be seen as a sign of hostility and humiliation. It is important to note that gifts are not always given by the rich to the poor. Even the poorest Ghanaian would like to give the only "valuable" item he or she has to a relatively rich person. A Danish volunteer and his wife once told the authors about a gift they received in a Ghanaian village on their day of departure after working with the local people for two years. A poor elderly woman knocked on their door early in the morning with two eggs in a small basket. When they opened the door she gave them the eggs saying, "Take them to Denmark to your family." This elderly woman's gesture clearly demonstrates the general Ghanaian attitude to gifts.

## AGE AND AUTHORITY

Like many other parts of Africa, age is an important factor in social interaction in Ghana. The general view is that elderly people have proved their strength in the face of all the disruptive forces in life and have lived in harmony with both the ancestral spirits and nature. That is why they are blessed with old age. Their wealth of experience carries with it natural authority and respect. Even a day's difference in age can be a decisive factor in interpersonal relationship. A younger person must show deep respect to a senior in age. The wider the age difference the greater the respect it commands. Disrespect for old people is taken as a serious offence.

The specific modes of respect differ with locality. Generally, younger people are expected to give their seats to their seniors in age. Children do not participate in conversations with their seniors unless they are directly addressed. In some areas, they do not stare their seniors in the face when they are spoken to. These rules must, however, not give the impression that children are pushed out of the daily lives of the grown-ups. Children eat, play and work together with their parents. As mentioned earlier, they are the most treasured values of Ghanaians and are therefore treated as such.

A young person's disobedience to the parents is a grave offence which can bring misfortune to the entire family. In tribes with matrilineal inheritance, a nephew's offence against his uncle is considered more serious than a son's against his father.

People in senior positions in business and public institutions expect their juniors and guests to accord them due respect. It is, for example, disrespectful to call your boss or host by the first name. Elderly men in towns and villages are also addressed by honorific titles such as *Nana, Togbui* or *Nii* meaning "elder man" in Akan, Ewe and Ga languages respectively. Women have similar honorific titles. For example, prefixes such as *auntie, mame* or *dada* are added to the names of young women when addressing them in Akan and Ewe languages respectively.

## CARING FOR THE AGED

In Western societies, the state has effectively assumed the responsibilities of taking care of their senior citizens. In Ghana, the responsibility falls on the younger generation. Despite the occasional problems that this entails, it remains one of the cherished values of the Ghanaian society, a value which the citizens are determined to preserve. It is an enshrined cultural belief that only children and relatives can give old people the love and care they need when their own energy is all spent. That is to say, the children repay their debts of gratitude to their parents for protecting and guiding them when they were still too young to care for themselves.

This multi-generational family care and ties have other values. As hinted earlier, they nourish the pool of Ghanaian moral wisdom and secure its transmission from one generation to the next. This ensures that moral widsom is learnt slowly and therefore properly understood. Gathering around grandparents and hearing stories of the past and about the life of their ancestors is still a favourite pastime for many village children in Ghana.

## THE CONCEPT AND ATTITUDE TO TIME

It is generally conceded in the anthropological literature that societies have different standards of time. This is reflected in definition of lateness, that is to say, the variation in time considered to be a decent behaviour when appointments are scheduled or the length of time allowed for an assignment. Time passes by unnoticingly in Ghana or is simply ignored. You do not expect a person to arrive on time when invited. If he finally comes, do not expect an apology. He has arrived, and that is what matters.

The Ghanaian's attitude to time remains the same irrespective of the seriousness of the event to which he has been invited. This frustrates and puzzles many foreigners. Business negotiations may be delayed because the negotiating team arrives several hours after the scheduled time. Invitations to dinners are treated in the same manner: "If you arrive on time your host might think you could not feed yourself for the evening and had to depend on his/her generosity," goes one explanation. Ghanaians themselves occasionally miscalculate each other's interpretation of time in informal agreements. As Daniel (1993 p.19) explains with humour, "It is very much like us to wait till a day to the time before we go to the dressmaker to be measured for the dress we want tomorrow. Naturally, the dress is not ready when tomorrow comes. What may have happened is that another customer came after us whose tomorrow sounded more urgent, who had more to offer for incentives, who stood guard over the dressmaker to ensure that he applied himself to the work in hand. One customer who could not mount guard called for collection a whole week after the date given him, but still came away empty-handed. To his complaints the dressmaker had a refrain, why did he not come when told?"

# CHAPTER 8

# Amusement and Festivals

## GHANAIAN MUSIC

Daily life in Ghana is generally bright and vivacious. Many visitors wonder about the sources of Ghanaian energy and joy, considering the obvious "poverty" that surrounds them. The "secret" lies in the Ghanaian culture from which the citizens derive their high-spirited attitude to life in general. "Never say despair" and "No condition is permanent" are favourite Ghanaian slogans, emphasizing the people's hope in the future.

This hope and determination is reflected in the various forms of entertainment found in the country, but most particularly in music. There is music for every aspect of life — joy and sorrow, work and play, war and peace as well as religious and secular life. Even every form of activity has its special music. Farmers, for example, have special songs for clearing, sowing, weeding and harvesting. Hunters have their own music. These work songs emphasize the prime value of cooperation and the coordination of human energies needed to forge a progressive community. Ghanaian music also comes in a wide range of varieties, with various levels of sophistication and community participation. As one moves from one locality to the other, one notices the influence of the various sub-cultures on the music and instruments people play and this adds yet another dimension to the musical variety and richness.

## Popular Music

For those who like night life, the major towns and cities of Ghana provide opportunities for memorable excitement. The night clubs, discos, and hotels swing with both local and Western music right from the afternoons (around 2 p.m.) to the early mornings (around 2 a.m). The variety is wide.

Ghana is known in West Africa as the centre of highlife music. From here this form of dance music has spread to many other West African countries from the beginning of the 1920s. Highlife music is a fusion of indigenous dance rhythms and melodies with influences from the West. The Western influences came during the World War years from Western soldiers stationed on the Guinea Coast, the African-American seamen, many centuries of church music as well as African adaptations of Western ballroom dance music. In its modern form, one notices traces of black American blues, Carribean reggae, as well as pop and rock music all blended in a unique African style. But despite the introduction of many Western musical instruments into the local bands, the African rhythms are distinctly preserved. The local hand drums, rattles and time-keeping instruments and many others still feature prominently.

At funerals, outdooring ceremonies, durbars and festivals, local bands are normally hired to play for the gathering. The Ga *Kpanlogo*, the Ewe *Borborbor*, the Dagomba *Simpa* and the Akan *Bosue* are examples of this form of popular music. One notices the influence of highlife musical styles on these traditional forms of music. But their local distinctiveness gives them a unique popularity. People from all social classes, and age groups dance to the music and share the joy of it.

## PERFORMING ARTS

Accra serves the amusement needs of theatre lovers. Plays are staged at the National Theatre, Centre for National Culture, the Drama Studio, and at the Institute of Performing Arts of the University of Ghana. Most of the plays are written by African authors and focus attention on important social, economic and political issues in Ghana as well as other parts of Africa. They are nearly always performed in English.

There are also comic theatre groups popularly known as Concert Parties who perform in the local languages. Their plays are normally performed with the accompaniment of indigenous music and dance. Unlike Western theatrical forms, there is a great deal of audience participation at these performances, in the form of applauding, weeping, jeering and throwing coins and notes on stage. Since such performances are in the local languages, visitors can only enjoy them fully if they understand the language or have good interpreters beside them.

### FESTIVALS

Apart from the daily musical experiences, several Ghanaian communities set aside a few days in a year for festivals. These festivals are of great social significance. They offer everybody in the community — both young and old — the opportunity to give a collective expression to their joy. The atmosphere at these festivals is always charged with the well known Ghanaian cheer and delight which sweep visitors off their feet at a go.

At these festivals one also gets a good opportunity to see a visible expression of Ghanaian culture in various forms. The participants are richly dressed in the colourful clothes (both modern and traditional), the paramount chief is dressed in royal regalia and carried in a palanquin. Mock military exercises and war dances are exhibited.

Ghanaian festivals today serve religious, social and developmental objectives. As will soon be discussed, most of the festivals have their roots in the traditional religious beliefs of the various communities. In addition to this, the festivals provide occasions for social reunion among Ghanaians. Relatives and friends see each other again, gifts and drinks are exchanged, disputes settled and an atmosphere of mutual cooperation established. Fur    more, the stories which are told and the rituals performed during the festivals remind members of the communities of their shared values and obligations. In more recent years, the festivals have created opportunities for smaller communities to invite national politicians to their areas and put before them their social and economic problems. Completed community development projects are commissioned and new ones launched with fund raising activities. There are two major types of annual community festivals. These are:

(i)  Harvest festivals (such as the yam festivals of the Ewe and the *Homowo* of the Ga), and

(ii) Festivals in memory of ancestors and past leaders (such as the *Adae* festivals of the Akan).

Many local festivals are held in various parts of the country at different times of the year. But we will concentrate only on the major types in this section. (A list of festivals and the months in which they are held is provided on p. 89 of this book for a quick reference).

As hinted above, each festival has significant religious values. Harvest festivals are based on the belief that the earthly gods have a tremendous influence on the physical environment and therefore determine the outcome of harvests. A good harvest is an indication of the full satisfaction and blessing of the gods. It is therefore natural to give them sincere thanks and to pray for their continual protection, before the community as a whole begins to enjoy the produce. A poor harvest on the other hand is an indication of the gods' dissatisfaction with the behaviour of certain individuals in the community. The community as a whole must be purified and the gods pacified in order to ensure good harvests in subsequent years.

Festivals held in memory of past leaders and outstanding ancestors reaffirm Ghanaians' belief in the eternity of life and the unbroken link between the living and the dead. As indicated earlier, ancestors are believed to be in a position to offer protection to the living against harmful spirits which might cause havoc in the community. In order to provide readers with some idea of how these festivals are held, we describe two of the most popular ones below.

## Adae Festival

The Adae festival is one of the principal annual festivals of the Akan. The word *Adae* literally means a resting place. But is has two meanings when used in connection with festivals. Firstly, it means a place where the spirits of departed chiefs are housed. A small wooden stool is usually carved for the spirit of each departed chief and these stools are kept in a sacred room called *Nkonguafieso*. Secondly, Adae also refers to the day of the month when the ruling chief and his elders enter the sacred room and offer thanks to the spirits for their protection.

The Akan divide their calendar year into nine 40-day cycles. During each cycle two Adaes are observed, one on Sunday called *Akwasidae*, and the other on Wednesday called *Awukudae*. The ninth Awukudae is set aside as a big annual festival called the *Odwira* festival in order to separate it from the other Adae ceremonies. Odwira is celebrated in such major Akan communities as Akim, Akuapem and Akwamu.

The eve of Adae is called *Dapaa*. All preparations for the festival must be completed on that day — foodstuffs, firewood, water, drinks, chicken, sheep, eggs and all other essentials for the celebration must be made ready. Visitors coming for the celebration are usually expected to arrive on that day. Drumming and dancing at the chief's house on the Dapaa evening marks the commencement of the Adae festival. In the early hours of the Adae day, the chief's principal drummers salute the spirits with their loud drums and bring sleeping villages back to life. The ceremonies of the day start in the sacred room of the spirits *(nkonguafieso)*. Before  entering the room, a calabashful of water is poured at the entrance. With this, the spirits are symbolically invited to wash their hands and prepare themselves for the feast. In the room, mashed yam or plantain is sprinkled on the stools by the chief while he recites words of praise to the spirits and invites them to eat. A sheep is also slaughtered and the stools smeared with the blood. The meat is later used in preparing a dish which is taken back  to the sacred room and placed before the stools.

The morning atmosphere is generally filled with extra briskness and excitement. The elders of the town return each other's visits, sharing morning drinks and wishing their family members the blessings of the gods and ancestral spirits. The town's master drummer and his assistants beat  the  talking drums from dawn to dusk. The various dancing groups in the town gather in their leaders' houses to go through their final preparations. Around noon people start gathering at the centre of the town for the climax of the festival — the durbar. Politicians and other invited guests also begin to arrive. The paramount chief and the elders are led in a procession through the principal streets to  the durbar grounds, cheered by a jubilating crowd. The durbar begins with the chief and his council of elders exchanging greetings with the invited guests. A great deal of the programme involves various forms of drumming and dancing with  the public joining  in  the dances. Politicians use  the occasion to address the community and inform the people about government plans. At the end of  the durbar,  the paramount chief is led home amidst continuous drumming, singing and dancing. The jubilation continues deep into the night.

## Homowo

This is the best known Ga festival. *Homowo* literally  means jeering and hooting at hunger. As tradition has it, severe famine broke out among the Ga many hundred years ago. It lasted for several years. When the rains returned there was a bumper harvest, and the people spontaneously hooted at the hunger that had plagued them for several years, demonstrating their joy and relief. This is the origin of Homowo. At the beginning of the rainy season each year, the seven principal priests in the Ga traditional area announce the start of the sowing season by a ritual sowing of corn. From that day, a ban is placed on drumming and dancing and other forms of noise-making throughout the area. The ban is lifted thirty days later, again with special ceremonies.

Homowo day falls in August, either on a Saturday (for Accra city) or on a Tuesday (i.e. ten days later) for those living in the suburbs of Osu, Labadi, Teshie, Nungua, Kpone, Prampram and Ningo. Tema people hold their festival on a Friday. The day prior to the festival is marked by brisk preparations. The Ga people living and working outside the Ga traditional area return to their ancestral home to join in the celebrations with their relatives. The travellers group themselves at the outskirts of the city and either walk or drive through the principal streets jubilating with songs.

The day after their arrival is the traditional yam festival and final preparations for the actual Homowo. The women mill the corn, buy palm oil, faggots and other ingredients for the big feast. The main gates of the houses are painted red, symbolically to drive away evil spirits. The children and the men join in the general cleaning, where their help is needed.

The main dish of the Homowo day is *kpokpoi* and palmnut soup. Kpokpoi is made from steamed unleavened corn dough mashed through pounding in a mortar. The corn dough is salted and mixed with palm oil. All cooking is done before midday. Some of the food is sprinkled around the doorsteps of every house for the ancestral spirits to partake in the feast. The spiritual heads of each community perform similar rites for the community gods and ancestors who have relatives alive. These rites are normally accompanied by drumming, singing and dancing. As a reminder of those famine days of the distant past, the males of each household scramble over a bowl of kpokpoi while the women watch and applaud. It is a spectacular sight to see both young and old men scramble over the dish — trying to beat each other in the art of finding the best morsel of fish in the bowl. The day following the Homowo festival is spent exchanging visits and greetings. It is a day to see life anew and to make amends where relations have been strained due to mis-understandings.

## FOOD

The largest hotels serve good international cuisine as well as Ghanaian dishes. There are also restaurants which serve Eastern, French and other European specialities. Among the best known eating places in Accra are  Le Bouquet, Novotel, Golden Tulip— all serving European dishes; Hirloon (Labone), Dynasty (Osu) —for Chinese dishes. Any taxi driver in the city can easily locate these restaurants.

But it will be a pity for a visitor to eat only  the interna-tional dishes which he/she knows too well. Naturally,  the memory of one's visit will be further enriched if one tries the wide variety of tropical fruits, vegetable and fresh water fish in Ghana and prepared in local style. Places where local dishes are served are: Country Kitchen, Providence (all at Osu) and Best Cuisine at Ridge. For fast foods, Papaye, Bus Stop, Afrikiko, Kikiriki are recommended.

Seen with Western eyes Ghanaian food is overcooked. It takes several hours to prepare palmnut or groundnut soup; some types of food like *kenkey* (made with maize) are cooked over a long period. As Ebow Daniel (1993 p.23) expresses it, "We are not known to serve the medium-rare, since the well-done is our forte, but there is no complaint as to palatability, only that we deny ourselves protein from too much cooking. For all the ailments concealed in animal and plant food of which we know little, it is perhaps just as well we do not spare the fire. We live to eat another day."

## Some Local Foodstuffs and Fruits

Plantain (a large, green, banana-like vegetable. Prepared in different ways — roasted, boiled or fried)

Cassava (*manioc*) (a commonly grown tuber, rich in carbohydrates)

Cocoyam (a large forest root, eaten roasted, fried or boiled. Cocoyam is also used in making *fufu*. Its leaves are used as spinach)

Okro (*okra*) (a tropical vegetable)

Guava (a small round tropical fruit whose taste reminds one of peach, but its seeds are like those of tomatoes. It can be eaten as dessert or used in preparing desserts, fruit salads, etc.)

Mango (a tropical fruit which appears like an irregular shaped pear in orange yellowish colour when ripe. It has a distinct flavour. Its major season is in December, just before Christmas)

Pawpaw (*papaya*) (a melon-type fruit. It is yellow when ripe and has black seeds. It is eaten separately as fruit or can be used in preparing fruit salads)

Others: Banana, Pineapple, Watermelon, Avocado Pear are all very popular tropical fruits which are commonly sold in the streets or at fruit stands.

# POPULAR GHANAIAN FESTIVALS

| Festival | Town/Area | Region | Month |
| --- | --- | --- | --- |
| Rice | Akpafu | Volta | January |
| Kpini-kyiu | Wa | Upper West | January |
| Tengbana | Tongu | Upper | January |
| Danso Abiam | Techimantia | Brong Ahafo | January |
| Ntoa Fokuokese | Nkoranza | Brong Ahafo | January |
| Yam | Kpedze | Volta | September |
| Volo | Volo | Volta | March |
| Hogbetsotso | Anlo | Volta | November |
| Lekoyi | Likpe | Volta | November |
| Lalue Kpledzo | Prampram | Eastern | March |
| Dipo | Manya Krobo | Eastern | March |
| Kotokyikyi | Senya Beraku | Central | March |
| Homowo | Accra | Gt. Accra | August |
| Asafotufiam | Ada | Gt. Accra | August |
| Papa | Kumawu | Ashanti | January |
| Apafram | Akwamu | Eastern | January |
| Aboakyer | Winneba | Central | May |
| Kundum | Nzima & Ahanta | Western | September |
| Akyempem | Agona | Ashanti | September |
| Bohyemhuo | Essumeja | Ashanti | November |
| Atweaban | Ntonso | Ashanti | November |
| Dam | Dagomba | Northern | April |
| Bugum | Dagomba | Northern | April |
| Don | Bolga | Upper | May |
| Wodomi | Yilo Krobo | Eastern | April |
| Wodomi | Manya Krobo | Eastern | July |
| Ahoba Kuma | Abura | Central | June |
| Odwira | Akuapem | Eastern | September |
| Eguado To | Abura | Central | August |
| Ahoba Kese | Abura | Central | August |
| Mafi Hogbetsotso | Adidome | Volta | December |
| Fetu | Cape Coast | Central | September |
| Ogyapa | Senya Beraku | Central | March |
| Apiba | Senya Beraku | Central | June |
| Kurubi | Nemase | Brong Ahafo | March |
| Apoo | Techiman | Brong Ahafo | March |
| Okyir | Nkusukum | Central | December |

# CHAPTER 9

# Places of Interest

Having gained some insight into the political, economic and historical events that have shaped the lives of Ghanaians over the past 1,000 years as well as the cultural values, norms and rituals that colour them, it is purposeful now to draw the reader's attention to some of the historical monuments and geographical evidence of these events and patterns of life.

## HISTORICAL MONUMENTS

As noted in earlier chapters, the first four centuries of European presence on the Gold Coast (as Ghana was then called) was marked by a vigorous construction of castles, forts and lodges. Out of some 60 recorded establishments only 20 are still in existence and a few of them are in usable conditions. Among them are the three castles which today constitute an invaluable part of the historical monuments of the country. These are the Elmina, the Christiansborg and the Cape Coast Castles.

During the colonial period they served as mini cities within which the laws of their European owners prevailed and from where the adjoining territories were administered and major business transactions were conducted. Today they remind us largely of the inhuman conditions under which slaves were kept as well as the battles fought among European trading powers in order to gain supremacy over each other. In some areas, the castles have served some useful developmental purposes as well. Being equipped with workshops in which the local inhabitants worked, they became important agents of technological change of that time. Many local artisans were trained in such crafts as carpentry, ship repairing and gardening. From them many new crops such as tomatoes and maize were also introduced into Ghana's agriculture.

In order to provide our readers with some idea of what to expect, we now describe the historical background and some of the distinctive features of the castles in greater detail.

## The Castles of Elmina

Elmina is a coastal town in what is now the Central Region of Ghana. It is reputed as having one  of the most attractive foreshores in West Africa, and was the centre of early European and Arabian trading activities on the Guinea Coast. The name Elmina is believed to originate either from the Arabic word *Al-Mina*, meaning "the harbour" or the Portuguese word *"a mina"* meaning "the mines" — a reference to the gold deposits believed to be in the area.

The first fort of Elmina was built by the Portuguese in 1482 and was named Fort San Jorge d'Elmina. It was later on rebuilt into a castle and became commonly known as the Elmina Castle.

The Portuguese chose Elmina as their trading station for a number of reasons. Firstly, it was very near to the sea — an important consideration at a time when sea transport was the main means of contact with the outside world. Secondly, it was close to a major gold deposit — gold was the major trading commodity at that time.

Increased inter-European competition and hostilities between the 15th and 16th centuries necessitated alterations and additional reinforcements to the castle. New bastions were constructed and the surrounding walls were made more solid and resistant to heavy cannon attacks. But in 1637 the Dutch captured it and remained its owners for over 200 years.

The intensive bombardments which preceded the capture seriously damaged the castle. The Dutch repaired the damage, made few additions and alterations aimed at improving its coastal defence capabilities.

On the hills just overlooking the Elmina Castle one sees another fort called Coenraadsburg or Fort St. Jago. This fort was built in 1638 by the Dutch to avoid an attack on the Elmina Castle from the hill top. The construction was first made with mud walls and were later fortified with stones. Under the Dutch, the fort served as a maintenance workshop and warehouse for goods meant for the Castle. It was sold (together with other Dutch possessions on the Gold Coast) to the British in 1872. The British made only a few alterations to the original Dutch construction.

Both the Castle and the fort are still in use. The Castle serves as a police training centre while the fort houses the headquarters of the Inspectorate Division of the Ghana Museums and Monuments Board. A generous collection of models, photographs and old prints of many of the forts and castles of Ghana are on display in the entrance lobby of the fort.

## Christiansborg Castle

The most important Danish establishment in Ghana is the Christiansborg Castle built at Osu, a suburb of Accra, in 1661 and named after the famous Danish King Christian IV. The Castle has a very interesting history. It started as a very simple square fort, built in stone in 1623, measuring approximately 20 metres along each curtain wall. When Danish trade began to flourish and competition among the European traders intensified, the fort was expanded into a castle and the entire building fortified to withstand cannon attacks. In addition to new living quarters and warehouses, the Castle also had prisons where slaves were kept for subsequent transportations to the plantations of America. Since the extensions to the fort were unplanned, the Castle came to assume an irregular shape, with its courtyard measuring 10 metres wide and 9.2 metres long. The events which shaped the first two hundred years of the castle's history were equally turbulent and unpredictable. In 1679 the Danish officer in charge of it was killed at the instigation of his Greek second-in-command. His successor sold the fort (as it then was) to a Portuguese governor who renamed it Fort Sao Francis Xavier. During the Portuguese occupation the curtain walls and bastions were raised by a metre and a chapel was built on the east side. The Danes negotiated with the king of Portugal and took the fort back in 1683. Two years later, it was mortgaged to the English who kept it for a brief period of four years at the end of which it was captured by the Akwamu. The Akwamu raid was led by a prominent trader by the name of Asameni who made himself governor, trading with the European governors on an equal footing.

A year later, the Danes paid 50 marks of gold to Asameni in return for the fort. During the succeeding sixty years the fort became the centre of Danish trade in gold and slaves. It was during this period that major extensions converted the fort into a castle. In 1850 the Danes sold the castle and all their other possessions to the British. From 1873 onwards (except for a brief period) the castle became the official residence of British governors on the Gold Coast. When the Gold Coast became independent in 1957 the new Prime Minister moved into it. It has since remained the official residence and/or office of the country's heads of government. The castle, is however, not opened to the public for security reasons and visitors must NOT take pictures in its vicinity if they are to avoid embarrassment from military personnel.

## Cape Coast Castle

The Cape Coast Castle has an interesting history as well. It was initially built as a fort by the Swedes in 1653 and named Carolusburg. In 1664 it was captured by the Dutch who kept it for a brief period, and lost it to the British in 1665. The fort is located in an area originally named Cabo Corso by the Portuguese, meaning "short cape". When the British gained trading control of the area, they corrupted the original name to Cape Coast. To meet the demands of a buoyant trade, the British reconstructed the fort into a castle, spreading the construction work over 18 years. It then became the headquarters of the British until 1876 when they moved their headquarters to Accra.

The castle now houses the West African Historical Museum which was opened in 1974 under the care of the University of Cape Coast. It has therefore become an important tourist attraction in the central region. Daily guide tours are organized and visitors are shown around the castle itself as well as the historical artifacts collected from different African countries. Some of the important historical sites and items shown are:

(i) The small slave prisons where up to 1, 500 slaves were kept for weeks, perhaps months before shipment.
(ii) The magazines for guns and gunpowder.
(iii) A clock made in 1861 which still functions.
(iv) Large cannons weighing three tons each, requiring 14 men to operate.

In the historical museum one can see clay figures, brass works and sculptures from various parts of West Africa. Notable among them are paintings and pictorial illustrations of the Anglo-Ashanti war of 1874, popularly known as the Sagrenti War, as well as portraits of commander Jan Pranger (Director General of the Elmina Castle 1730–1734) and his wife.

OTHER PLACES OF INTEREST

## Boti Falls

A natural water fall located near Huhunya in the Eastern region. It is about 30 metres high and falls at the speed of 25 km per second.

## Aburi Gardens

Aburi Botanical Gardens — located on the Akuapem Hills, about 30 minutes' drive from Accra. The gardens contain a wide variety of tropical plants carefully arranged and cared for. It is also a beautiful relaxation spot, away from the bustling city life.

## Kumasi —"the Garden City"

Kumasi is the main city and regional capital of the Ashanti region, and has its special attractions. It is called the "garden city" due to its attractive valleys. It has other attractions including the Ghana National Cultural Centre — a combination of museum, open air theatre, craft workshops, art gallery, model farm and zoo. It also houses one of the country's three universities, the University of Science and Technology, surrounded by a tropical scenic beauty.

## Bonwire — Home of *Kente*

Bonwire lies a few kilometres away from Kumasi. It is a popular handicraft centre — noted mainly for its beautiful traditional textile designs and weaving. The best known of them is the *kente* cloth. Each kente is a distinct piece of art work in very rich colours. The weaving is done by hand using a traditional technique which is over three centuries old.

## Akosombo

Apart from being the location of the Volta Dam, Akosombo offers modern facilities for recreation. There is a yacht club, a filtered swimming pool and a modern hotel from the top of which one enjoys a beautiful view of the dam and the surrounding towns.

From here the visitor can also travel with the *Akosombo Queen* on the Volta Lake right to Yapei near Tamale in northern Ghana.

## Tamale's Traditional Architecture

The northern part of the country has its particular fascinations. The vegetation, the climate and the culture are very different from the south. The largest town in the area is Tamale which can be reached by road from Kumasi or by air from Accra. Tamale's tourist attractions include its markets, and its traditional architecture (particularly the mosque).

## The Mole National Park

From Tamale one can continue northwards to Bolgatanga and then to Burkina Faso. One can also go westwards to see the Mole National Park at Damongo, where trained guides are on the wait to take the visitor round at his/her request. The Park also has a modern hotel high above a water hole and provides an excellent position for game viewing. From Damongo the tour can go to Wa where the visitor sees other examples of fascinating traditional architecture, especially the dazzling white palace of the chief.

## The Crocodile Pond at Paga

There is also a famous crocodile pond in Paga which lies north west of Bolgatanga. The local people can entice the crocodiles out of the pond and play with them.

### GENERAL GUIDELINES FOR A GOOD TRAVELLER

Travel in a spirit of humility and with a genuine desire to learn more about the people of your host country.

Be sensitively aware of the feelings of other people, thus preventing what can be an offensive behaviour on your part. (This applies very much to photography.)

Cultivate the habit of listening and observing, rather than merely hearing and seeing.

Be aware that very often people in the country you visit have time concepts and thought patterns different from your own. This does not make them inferior, only different.

Instead of looking for that "beach paradise" discover the enrichment of seeing different ways of life, through other eyes.

Acquaint yourself with local customs — people will be happy to help you.

Instead of the Western practice of "knowing all the answers" cultivate the habit of asking questions.

Remember that you are only one of the thousands of travellers visiting the country and do not expect special privileges.

Do not make promises to the local people during your visit unless you are certain you can carry them through.

Spend time reflecting on your daily experiences in an atttempt to deepen your understanding.

Be polite and always ask before taking photographs of anyone. Avoid taking pictures of anything which could be regarded to be of military importance. This includes the airport and soldiers.

Respect your host country's attitude to dressing and decency. Avoid dressing in a manner that may label you a "hippie". Women must cover the thighs up to the knees and avoid going in bare tops. Nudism is not permitted on the beaches or in the streets of Ghana.

## FOR FURTHER READING

Abban, J. B. *Prerequisites of Manpower and Educational Planning in Ghana*. Accra: Baafour Educational Enterprises Ltd, 1986.

Ammah, Charles. *Ga Homowo and Other Ga-Adangme Festivals*. Accra: Sedco 1985.

Arhin, Kwame. *Traditional Rule in Ghana: Past and Present*. Accra: Sedco, 1985.

Assimeng, Max. *Social Structure of Ghana*. Accra: Ghana Publishing Corporation, 1981.

Birmingham, Walter *et al* (eds): *A Study of Contemporary Ghana*, Vols. 1&2 Evanston: North West University Press, 1966.

Dantzig, Albert van. *Forts and Castles of Ghana*. Accra: Sedco, 1980.

Ephson, Issac S. *Ancient Forts and Castles of the Gold Coast*. Accra: Ilen Chambers, 1970.

Gullestrup, Hans. *Kultur, Kulturanalyse og Kulturetik*. Denmark: Akademisk forlag, 1992.

Hofstede, Gert. *Cultures and Organizations: Soft Ware of the Mind*. England: McGraw-Hill Book Company, 1991.

Kuada, John E. *Managerial Behaviour in Ghana and Kenya — A Cultural Perspective*. Denmark: Aalborg University Press, 1994.

Loxley, John. *Ghana: Economic Crisis and the Long Road to Recovery*. Ottawa: The North-South Institute, 1988.

Ministry of Information *Ghana '76 — An Official Handbook*. Accra: Ghana Information Service Department, 1976.

National Museum of Ghana: *A Handbook*. Tema: Ghana Publishing Corporation, 1973.

National Museum of Ghana: *Christiansborg Castle — Osu*. Accra: Ministry of Information, 1970.

Opoku, A. A. *Festivals of Ghana*. Tema: Ghana Publishing Corporation, 1970.

Sarpong, Peter *Ghana in Retropspect: Some Aspects of Ghanaian Culture*. Accra: Ghana Publishing Corporation, 1974.

Toye, John. "Structural Adjustment: Context, Assumptions, Origin and Diversity." *Poverty and Development,* no. 11. Ministry of Foreign Affairs, the Development Cooperation Information Department, The Hague, 1994.

Twumasi, P. A. *Medical Systems in Ghana. A Study in Medical Sociology.* Tema: Ghana Publishing Corporation, 1975.

# Index

102